THE ROOTS OF PLATONISM

The Origins and Chief Features of a Philosophical Tradition

How does a school of thought, in the area of philosophy, or indeed of religion, from roots that may be initially open-ended and largely informal, come to take on the features that later mark it out as distinctive, and even exclusive? That is the theme which is explored in this book in respect of the philosophical movement known as Platonism, stemming as it does from the essentially open-ended and informal atmosphere of Plato's Academy. John Dillon focuses on a number of key issues, such as monism versus dualism, the metaphysical underpinnings of ethical theory, the theory of Forms, and the reaction to the sceptical 'deviation' represented by the so-called 'New Academy'. The book is written in the lively and accessible style of the lecture series in Beijing from which it originates.

JOHN DILLON is Regius Professor of Greek (Emeritus) at Trinity College Dublin. His chief publications are *The Middle Platonists* (1977; 2nd ed. 1996); *Iamblichus, De Anima* (with John Finamore; 2000); *Alcinous: The Handbook of Platonism* (1993); *The Heirs of Plato* (2003); and three volumes of collected essays. In 2004 he was awarded the Gold Medal of the Royal Irish Academy for distinguished research in the Humanities.

THE ROOTS OF PLATONISM

PLATONISM

The Origins and Chief Features of a Philosophical Tradition

JOHN DILLON

Trinity College, Dublin

CAMBRIDGE
UNIVERSITY PRESS

CAMBRIDGE
UNIVERSITY PRESS

Shaftesbury Road, Cambridge CB2 8EA, United Kingdom

One Liberty Plaza, 20th Floor, New York, NY 10006, USA

477 Williamstown Road, Port Melbourne, VIC 3207, Australia

314–321, 3rd Floor, Plot 3, Splendor Forum, Jasola District Centre, New Delhi – 110025, India

103 Penang Road, #05–06/07, Visioncrest Commercial, Singapore 238467

Cambridge University Press is part of Cambridge University Press & Assessment, a department of the University of Cambridge.

We share the University's mission to contribute to society through the pursuit of education, learning and research at the highest international levels of excellence.

www.cambridge.org
Information on this title: www.cambridge.org/9781108446884

DOI: 10.1017/9781108584906

First published 2019
First paperback edition 2024

A catalogue record for this publication is available from the British Library

Library of Congress Cataloging-in-Publication data
NAMES: Dillon, John M., author.
TITLE: The Roots of Platonism : The Origins and Chief Features of a Philosophical Tradition / John Dillon.
DESCRIPTION: Cambridge, United Kingdom ; New York, NY : Cambridge University Press, 2019. | Includes bibliographical references and index.
IDENTIFIERS: LCCN 2018015845 | ISBN 9781108426916
SUBJECTS: LCSH: Platonists. | Philosophy, Ancient.
CLASSIFICATION: LCC B517 .D555 2018 | DDC 184–dc23
LC record available at https://lccn.loc.gov/2018015845

ISBN   978-1-108-42691-6   Hardback
ISBN   978-1-108-44688-4   Paperback

To my grandsons,
Kian and Bobby

Contents

Preface

The present volume takes its start from a set of six lectures delivered to the Department of Philosophy of Renmin University in Beijing during the last two weeks of October 2016, as the eighth in an ongoing series of Master Classes in Ancient Greek Philosophy. I am most grateful to Professor Wei Liu of the Department for the original invitation, and for copious hospitality during my stay. A version of the lectures is due to be published in due course in Chinese translation. The original lectures have been considerably revised for the present edition, and I am greatly indebted to Michael Sharp of Cambridge University Press for accepting my proposal to turn a set of somewhat disconnected papers into a book, and to the two anonymous readers that he selected for many useful suggestions as to achieving that goal. The remaining inadequacies are my own. Michael Sharp's original proposal to me was actually for a more comprehensive volume, surveying developments in the field of later Platonism in the forty years or so since the publication of my initial foray into the field, *The Middle Platonists*, in 1977, but I found that that was rather more than I could face, especially as there is now a plethora of younger scholars in the field who could do a better job on that than I. Instead, I thought that I would focus on certain salient aspects of the growth of the Platonist philosophical tradition, which is what chiefly interests me at the moment, and offer these essays as a contribution to that, as well as to further scholarly discussion on the subject.

A number of these essays had seen the light of day before being taken to China, and I am grateful to the editors of *Etudes platoniciennes* VIII, Alexandra Michalewski and Pieter d'Hoine, for permission to reproduce 'The Ideas as Thoughts of God', first delivered at a pleasant conference in Paris in 2009; to the publishers Steiner Verlag of Stuttgart, in respect of the essay on 'The Hierarchy of Being as a Framework for Platonist Ethical Theory', which originally formed part of a volume of essays on Platonist ethical theory, *Ethik des antiken Platonismus,* edited by Christian Pietsch, of the University of Münster, as a subsidiary to the completion of Volume VIII of the great enterprise *Der Platonismus in der Antike,* bequeathed to him by his predecessor in the chair, my old friend Matthias Baltes; and lastly to Wayne Hankey, editor of that excellent journal *Dionysius,* for permission to republish my paper 'Carneades the Socratic', which had originally seen the light of day as a Memorial Lecture in honour of Gregory Vlastos, at Queen's University, Kingston, Ontario, in September 2014 – another very pleasant occasion. I trust that the resulting volume achieves at least the modicum of coherence that I have tried to bestow upon it. *Habent sua fata libelli.*

A word about the cover image. I realise full well that the face peering out from amongst the roots is not that of Plato, but of the Buddha. Nonetheless, the picture seemed otherwise so apt that the Editor and I decided to adopt it, *faute de mieux,* since we could not alter it! There is an analogy, after all, with the development of the various Buddhist systems that is not irrelevant.

Acknowledgements

The author wishes to acknowledge with thanks permissions to republish material contained in Chapters 3, 4, 5 and 6 from the following: *Etudes platoniciennes,* for the contents of Chapter 3; Steiner Verlag of Stuttgart, for the contents of Chapter 4; *Dionysius,* for the contents of Chapter 5; and Cambridge University Press, for the contents of Chapter 6 (previously published as Chapter 10, 'Aporetic Elements in Plutarch's Philosophy', in George Karamanolis and Vasilis Politis (eds.), *The Aporetic Tradition in Ancient Philosophy,* 2018).

Introduction

The present work addresses a topic which has been of interest to me for some considerable time, to wit, the process by which the intellectual speculations pursued by Plato in the (rather informal) institution that he set up in the Academy park on the outskirts of Athens in around 387 BCE, and that he presided over until his death forty years later, came to assume the nature of a philosophical *system*. This is a question that I addressed first over thirty years ago now, in a paper entitled 'Self-Definition in Later Platonism',[1] where I set out to investigate, in the case of the Platonic School in particular, what provokes a philosophic or religious movement to define itself formally, in the sense of establishing an 'orthodoxy', and discerning 'heresies'. I pursued this question further in a later essay, '"Orthodoxy" and "Eclecticism": Middle Platonists and Neo-Pythagoreans',[2] in either case drawing what I suppose is the rather obvious conclusion that a philosophical school tends to define itself initially by reason of attacks made upon it by rivals, or indeed in the process of attacking those rivals: in the case of the Old Academy, this arises initially in response to attacks from Aristotle and the Peripatos; while in the case of the New Academy, it is the accompaniment of attacks by Arcesilaus and his successors on the rival Stoic school, who had contrived to 'corner the market' in the area of epistemological certainty, following on from the dogmatic system that had progressively arisen in the Old Academy.[3]

---

[1] First published in Meyers & Sanders (eds.) (1982), pp. 60–75; repr. in Dillon (1990).
[2] First published in Long & Dillon (eds.) (1988), pp. 103–25; repr. in Dillon (1997b). The inverted commas in the title are intended to be significant!
[3] I should specify here what I hope will become clear from the succeeding chapters, namely that the 'orthodoxy' being discussed here should be distinguished – as a 'weak' orthodoxy, let us

In the later 'Middle Platonic' period (viz. *c.* 100 CE), inter-school struggles seem to become somewhat less severe, but still Plutarch directs various polemics against both Stoics and Epicureans, while, later in the second century, Atticus strongly attacks the Peripatetics, apparently provoked by some rather patronizing remarks on the part of a Peripatetic rival, Aristocles of Messene, who composed a work *On Philosophy,* in ten books,[4] and who had dared, while commending Plato as quite a good philosopher for his time, to present him merely as a suitable *precursor* of the more perfect philosophy of Aristotle. Such impertinences cannot go unpunished! One can also observe, in the case of Atticus' approximate contemporary, Numenius of Apamea, both a vigorous, and entertainingly satirical, attack on the scepticism of the New Academy (with a sideswipe also at Antiochus of Ascalon), and an assertion of the essential role of Pythagoras as the true 'founding father' of Platonism – a tendency that goes back at least to Eudorus of Alexandria, in the later first century BCE, but even, to some extent at least, to Speusippus and Xenocrates in the Old Academy.

The six chapters (originally distinct papers)[5] presented here seek to contribute to this theme of developing self-definition and orthodoxy in various ways. In the first, 'The Origins of Platonist Dogmatism', I address in a general way the process by which, initially under the headship of Xenocrates, the third head of the Academy, but with modifications and amplifications on the part of his successor Polemon, a definitive set of doctrines seems to arise in the three fields of philosophy specified by him, Ethics, Physics and Logic, by contrast with the procedure of Plato himself, who, I argue, was more concerned with the free exploration of philosophical problems, such

---

say, as opposed to a 'strong' orthodoxy – from the kind of orthodoxy imposed by a centralized bureaucratic structure, such as arises, for example, in the various 'Abrahamic' religions. Within the Platonic tradition, there is really no centralized structure that could impose such uniformity of doctrine, even if there were a desire to do so. Instead, there is a certain spectrum of doctrinal positions which a Platonist can hold – which is not to say that he may not be challenged on these, either by colleagues or by successors. All that I see Xenocrates as doing is setting up certain parameters.

[4] Passages from whose work Eusebius quotes in the *Praeparatio Evangelica,* just prior to his quotations from Atticus.

[5] Earlier versions of three of these have appeared elsewhere: Chapter 3, in *Etudes platoniciennes* VIII (2011), pp. 31–42; Chapter 4 in *Ethik des antiken Platonismus,* hrsg. von C. Pietsch. Steiner Verlag: Stuttgart, 2013, pp. 91–8; and Chapter 5 in *Dionysius* 34 (2016), pp. 27–45.

as those of unity and plurality in the composition of the universe, the status of mathematical entities and generic and specific archetypes of physical individuals, and the nature and objective reality of ethical norms – the only restriction being the observance of a set of essentially *negative* conditions, well defined by Lloyd Gerson, in his most stimulating book, *From Plato to Platonism*[6]: that is to say, anti-materialism, anti-mechanism, anti-nominalism, anti-relativism, and anti-scepticism, which, cumulatively, can be seen to add up to a 'Platonist' stance in philosophy, termed by Gerson 'Ur-Platonism', or 'Fundamental Platonism'. What I see Xenocrates, in particular, as doing is both initiating a process of the exegesis of Plato's works, with the aim of reconciling any apparent contradictions or inconsistencies within the corpus (which he himself will have been the first to assemble), and composing a set of treatises on all or most of the main topics of philosophy, in order to provide an appropriate dogmatic underpinning to the corpus.

I turn next, with 'Monist and Dualist Tendencies in Platonism before Plotinus', to a basic question which has concerned later followers of Plato, both ancient and modern, namely whether his metaphysical system is essentially monist or dualist. Plato himself, as I note, provides plausible material in support of either alternative, and indeed his later follower Plutarch (who has something of an agenda of his own) comes out strongly in favour of Platonic dualism. Nonetheless, on balance, my conclusion is that Plato did not intend to set up a positive force of evil or disorder in opposition to his supreme unitary principle; rather, the secondary principle of multiplicity and diversity, the Indefinite Dyad, is best seen as complementary to the Monad (or One, or Good), and necessary for the generation of an ordered cosmos.

Likewise, the 'Receptacle' of the *Timaeus,* the 'ancient disharmony' of the *Statesman* myth, and the 'soul of the opposite capacity' of *Laws* X – all fastened upon as evidence by such a later dualist as Plutarch, are best seen, despite appearances, not as manifestations of a primordially existent 'disorderly World-Soul', but rather as essentially negative phenomena, inevitable concomitants of the generation

---

[6] Gerson (2013), esp. pp. 9–32.

of a three-dimensional, material world, lying ready to hand for the ordering power of an essentially omnipotent first principle.

A third basic topic on this theme is that of the nature and situation of the Platonic system of Forms, or Ideas, those intelligible archetypes of particular objects, qualities and concepts that Plato judged to be essential (in view of the fluid and evanescent nature of physical particulars) for the establishment of an ordered cosmos, and the attaining of secure knowledge (as opposed to opinion), allowing for the existence of rational and coherent discourse. I do not here venture to take on the vast question concerning 'of what things there are Forms', or as to what sort of *resemblance* there can be between a Form and its dependent particulars, interesting though these issues are. Instead, in 'The Ideas as Thoughts of God', I focus on an issue which has long been made something of a mystery in Platonic studies, namely where may we suppose the Forms or Ideas to reside. Plato himself makes the aged Parmenides dismiss the theory that they can be simply thoughts in the human mind (*Parmenides* 132B–C), as that would make them too subjective (they must be thoughts of *something*), but this does not preclude their being thoughts in the mind of God, as that would be the ultimate objective reality.

When we survey the revived dogmatic Platonism of the first century BCE, in the persons of Antiochus of Ascalon, Eudorus of Alexandria – and indeed the Jewish philosopher Philo of Alexandria – we find the Ideas as thoughts of God an established doctrine (reinforced by the assimilation to it of the Stoic doctrine of divine *logoi*). I want here to suggest, however, that this is not to be seen as an innovation of that period (one gets no sense from any of the figures here mentioned that they think that they are innovating in propounding this doctrine), but rather as a doctrine descending to them from the Old Academy, and specifically from Xenocrates, for whom the supreme principle was a Monad which is also an Intellect (*nous*) – and an intellect must necessarily have thoughts! I would suggest further, indeed, that, once one had resolved on a 'de-mythologizing' exegesis of Plato's *Timaeus,* as do both Speusippus and Xenocrates, the 'Paradigm', or Model, in accordance with which the Demiurge fashions the physical world, can in consequence be regarded as nothing else than the contents of his intellect – he now in effect becoming a rational World-Soul.

In the later 'Middle Platonic' period, it must be said, after the time of Plutarch, it became an issue as to whether the Forms or Ideas should be regarded as being inside or outside the divine Intellect, as being internal to it must have come to seem a compromise of their objective reality, and Plotinus has to engage in a protracted argument on this subject with his pupil Porphyry, who has come to him from the Athenian school of Longinus, with Plotinus ultimately converting him to the doctrine that the Forms are *within* Intellect – but then this intellect becomes a secondary divinity, lower than the One, which transcends thought.

Turning now to the sphere of Ethics, the fourth issue that I propose to address, in 'The Hierarchy of Being as a Framework for Platonist Ethical Theory', is that of the way that ethical theory in the Platonic tradition is tied in with metaphysics, and in particular how the *telos,* or 'end of goods', is related to the concept of the divinity. Starting with Antiochus of Ascalon, and then passing through Eudorus and Plutarch to Alcinous, I am concerned to show how the two interconnected ideals of 'living in accordance with nature' (*homologoumenôs têi physei zên*) – originally Stoic, but appropriated by Antiochus – and 'assimilating oneself to God' (*homoiôsis theôi*) are dependent on a particular view of the nature of God and of our capacity to assimilate ourselves to him through the practice of the virtues.

Next, turning to a phase of the Platonist tradition which I have in general refrained from discussing in the past, the so-called New Academy – mainly because I tended to view it, as it is often viewed, as rather a part of the history of ancient Scepticism than of Platonism – I address, in 'Carneades the Socratic', that remarkable figure, Carneades of Cyrene, the last major figure in the 'New-Academic' school, with whom the later Platonist Plutarch, as we shall see, is prepared to claim an affinity, but who would have been rejected, along with his predecessor Arcesilaus, by the general body of later Platonists as 'heretics', to examine the respects in which he can be seen to be returning, like Arcesilaus before him, to the 'Socratic' aporetic roots of the Platonist tradition, while nevertheless postulating a certain degree of certainty, or at least 'probability' (*pithanotes*), in the cognition of the perceptible world, a degree of 'knowledge' for which, I argue, he could claim Socratic antecedents, despite Plato's own downplaying of the reliability of sensory impressions. Here, I make considerable use of the insights of the great Platonist scholar Gregory Vlastos (in whose honour this paper was originally produced) as to the distinctive degree of 'modified' knowledge which Socrates can be seen to claim, in various of the early dialogues, such as the *Apology* or the *Gorgias*.

Following on from this, and moving to a somewhat later stage in the development of the Platonic tradition, in the essay 'Plutarch's Relation to the New-Academic Tradition', I turn to the distinctive stance of the Middle Platonist Plutarch of Chaeroneia in relation to the 'sceptical' tradition of the New Academy of Arcesilaus and Carneades, as a segment of the Platonic tradition which was, as we have seen, generally rejected as heretical by Platonists from Antiochus on, but which Plutarch is prepared to embrace as a valid aspect of the heritage of Socrates. On the one hand, Plutarch embraces the aporetic, or 'questioning', tradition, which raises difficulties for the dogmatism of Stoic epistemology; and on the other hand, he seeks to deny that the New Academics practised a thorough-going scepticism of the Pyrrhonian variety. He sees them rather as training their pupils' minds by analysing the contradictions inherent in Stoic empiricism.

To illustrate Plutarch's approach, I examine first some sections of his polemic against the Epicurean Colotes (who himself was attacking Arcesilaus); then the first, and most programmatic, of his *Platonic Questions* in which he sets forth the position of Socrates, as he sees it; and lastly, the interesting little treatise *On the Principle of Cold*, addressed to his avowedly New-Academic follower Favorinus of Arles, showing him (somewhat ironically, I feel) how one should approach such a doubtful physical question as the nature of cold.

All in all, I hope to have presented in these six essays an overview of how doctrine within a philosophical school develops, and of the various turns that may be taken, and controversies that may arise, within the tradition. I am not aspiring, especially in view of the considerable stream of works on this general topic that have emerged in recent years, to provide here any sort of definitive study, but rather a contribution to the on-going debate as to the nature and origins of the Platonist tradition.

CHAPTER I

The Origins of Platonist Dogmatism

We may start our investigations with something of a general survey of the topic, highlighting the chief respects in which Plato's philosophical investigations progressively become something that we can reasonably term 'Platonism'. We can then proceed to focus on a series of key issues which together serve to delineate the parameters of this great tradition.

The philosopher Plato, as all his friends would agree, was a man of strong views on most subjects, but it is a notable fact that, in his published works, he chooses to present these views in a distinctly devious way. The Platonic dialogue, after all, is a literary form designed to advance philosophical positions *aporetically* and *dialectically,* not dogmatically. If we derive doctrines from them, it is, so to speak, at our own risk.[1]

Nonetheless there is indubitably a body of doctrine associated with the Platonic School. Even within Plato's own lifetime, we have the (admittedly tendentious) testimony of Aristotle as to the existence of certain philosophical principles of Plato which he on occasion[2] terms *agrapha dogmata,* and which have come to be known as the 'unwritten doctrines'. I have taken up a certain position on these myself,[3] seeking to strike a judicious balance between what I would regard as

---

[1] There is indeed a large and reasonably respectable body of opinion among Plato scholars which maintains that it is impossible to recover Platonic doctrine with any certainty from the dialogues; cf. e.g. the essays collected by Gerald Press (2000) and Charles Griswold (1988).

[2] E.g. *Metaph.* A 6, 987b29ff. A useful collection both of Aristotelian passages and of Neoplatonic commentaries on them is to be found in Krämer (1964).

[3] Dillon (2003), Chapter 1: 'The Riddle of the Academy'. For an incisive critique of the whole 'Tübingen' approach to the *agrapha dogmata,* see Mann (2006). I am indebted to Professor Pavel Gregoric for reminding me of this essay.

the extreme views of Harold Cherniss and his followers, such as
Leonardo Tarán, on the one hand, and the 'Tübingen School' of
Konrad Gaiser, Hans-Joachim Krämer, and *their* followers (such as
Giovanni Reale), on the other. To summarize my position here, I see
no problem about there being a body of doctrines, or at least working
hypotheses, which do not find their way into the dialogues, except in
devious and allusive forms, and that these doctrines, such as that of
the derivation of all things from a pair of first principles. A One and
an Indefinite Dyad should be of basic importance to Plato's system;
but I see no need, on the other hand, to hypothesize a full body of
secret lore, present in the Academy from its inception, which is
preserved as a sort of 'mystery' for the initiated.

Short of this, however, it seems to me entirely probable that a great
deal of philosophical speculation went on in the Academy which does
not find its way into a dialogue. After all, Plato never promises to
reveal his whole mind in writing – very much the opposite, indeed, if
one bears in mind such a text as *Phdr.* 275D–E, or the following
notable passage of the *Seventh Letter* (341C–E):[4]

> But this much I can certainly declare concerning all these writers, or
> prospective writers, who claim to know the subjects which I seriously
> study (*peri hôn egô spoudazô*), whether as having heard them from me
> or from others, or as having discovered them themselves; it is impos-
> sible, in my judgement at least, that these men should understand
> anything about this subject. *There does not exist, nor will there ever
> exist, any treatise of mine dealing therewith.* For it does not at all admit
> of verbal expression like other studies, but, as a result of continued
> application to the subject itself and actually living with it, it is brought
> to birth in the soul all of a sudden (*exaiphnês*), as light that is kindled
> by a leaping spark, and thereafter it nourishes itself.

Even if this is not Plato himself talking, as I say – though I believe it
is – it is surely someone who was well acquainted with the situation
obtaining in the school. Plato never really gave up on the Socratic
idea that philosophy must always be a primarily oral activity, and also
an open-ended process. So talk and argumentation prevailed in the
groves of the Academy. And the members of the Academy of whom

---

[4] Which I would certainly regard as authoritative (that is to say, emanating from sources in the
Old Academy who knew what they were talking about), even if its provenance from the hand
of Plato himself is disputed. (Unless otherwise attributed, translations are my own.)

we have any knowledge – figures such as Speusippus, Xenocrates, Aristotle, Eudoxus of Cnidus, or Heraclides of Pontus – were a pretty talkative and argumentative bunch; not the sort of people to sit around until Plato had completed another dialogue!

At any rate, whatever the status of these 'unwritten doctrines', we are, it seems to me, left with the interesting problem that, from the perspective of the later Platonist tradition, beginning with Antiochus of Ascalon in the first century BCE, a firm conviction arose that Plato and the Old Academy had put forth a consistent and comprehensive body of doctrine on all aspects of philosophy, and this belief continued throughout later antiquity. Not that Platonism was ever seen to be a monolithic structure; there was room for a fairly wide spectrum of positions on most ethical and physical questions. But there was a solid consensus that Plato *did* dogmatize, and did not, as the New Academicians, from Arcesilaus to Carneades, maintained, simply raise problems and suspend judgement.[5] What I would like to enquire into on this occasion is (a) whether there might be any justification for this belief and (b), if there is, at what stage might this dogmatism have arisen.

It seems to me best, in approaching this question, to start at the end, so to speak – that is, with the evidence of Antiochus of Ascalon – and work back. What we find with Antiochus – or rather, in a number of significant texts of Cicero, in which his spokespersons are expounding Platonic doctrine along Antiochian lines[6] – is, first of all, a clear division of the subject-matter of philosophy into the three domains of ethics, physics (including what we would consider rather 'metaphysics', or the discussion of first principles), and logic, and then a set

---

[5] Cf. the discussion of the question at the beginning of the *Anonymous Theaetetus Commentary*, a work emanating possibly from the late first century BCE, but more probably from the following century. As regards the New Academy, indeed, an interesting belief arose in later times (doubtless a pious fiction) that the New Academics did not believe this themselves, but only maintained this position in public to combat the Stoics, while dogmatizing in private! Cf. Sextus Empiricus *PH* 1.234 and August. *C. Acad.* 3. 20, 43 (quoting a lost section of Cicero's *Academica*).

[6] We are concerned chiefly with such works as *De Finibus* 4 and 5 (for ethics), and the *Academica Priora* and *Academica Posteriora* (for 'physics'), but there are a number of other significant passages also. For a fairly comprehensive treatment of Antiochus, see Dillon (1977), Chapter 2; but also, in a more sceptical mode, Barnes (1989); and now Sedley (ed.) (2012).

of confidently proclaimed doctrines, under each of those heads. It has long been assumed, without much dissent, that this construction is very largely a fantasy of Antiochus, concocted by dint of extrapolating back onto his heroes in the Old Academy a body of doctrine largely gleaned from the Stoics, by whose teachings he was deeply influenced.

I entered a plea against this assumption in *The Middle Platonists*, some forty years ago now, arguing on the one hand that there was little point in Antiochus trying to put over on a fairly sceptical and well-informed public a claim for which there was no justification whatever,[7] and on the other hand recalling how little we really know of doctrinal developments within the Old Academy, especially under the leadership of Xenocrates and Polemon. I was still, however, in that work pretty wary of attributing too much in the way of doctrine to Polemon in particular, since we seemed to know so little about him, despite his near-forty-year tenure of the headship. But since then I have been much encouraged by a most perceptive article of David Sedley's, 'The Origins of Stoic God', published in 2002,[8] which, it seems to me, opens the way to recovering much of Polemon's doctrinal position, and I have rather taken this ball and run with it, I'm afraid, in Chapter 4 of *The Heirs of Plato*.

I will return to David Sedley's article presently, but for the moment I want to concentrate rather on the topic of ethics, and even before that to focus on the question of the formal division of philosophy into topics at all, which seems to me to be bound up with the establishment of a philosophical *system*. We learn from Sextus Empiricus, in fact (*Adv. Log.* 1.16), that the first philosopher formally to distinguish the three main areas or topics of philosophy, which Sextus names in the order 'Physics – Ethics – Logic' but which can

---

[7] He is never, as I pointed out, accused of anything like this by Cicero, who himself, despite his great personal affection and respect for Antiochus, maintains a position loyal to the New Academy. All that Cicero accuses him of is being himself too close to the Stoics (*si perpauca mutavisset, germanissimus Stoicus, Acad. Post.* 132; *a Chrysippo pedem nusquam, Acad. Post.* 143; and cf. also *Acad. Pr.* 135, where Cicero seeks to nail him on the particular point of virtue being sufficient for happiness, which he declares was *not* the view of the Old Academy). All this, I maintain, does not amount to a dismissal of Antiochus' overall project – and it is, in any case, inter-school polemic.

[8] In Frede & Laks (2002), pp. 41–83.

occur in virtually any order, was Xenocrates.[9] However – and, I think, significantly – Sextus precedes this announcement by saying that Plato himself had already made this division 'virtually' (*dynamei*), since he discussed many problems in all these fields.[10] The true significance of this statement, I think, is that Xenocrates himself, in making this formal division, sought to father the concept on Plato himself, possibly in his attested work *On Philosophy* (Diog. Laert. *VP* 4.13). He could, after all, without difficulty have adduced various passages from the dialogues, and indeed whole dialogues, such as the *Timaeus,* for physics, *Republic* 4 for ethics, or the *Theaetetus* for epistemology (as part of logic) – or indeed the second part of the *Parmenides* in the same connection – which would support his contention, very much as is done by later composers of Platonist handbooks, such as Alcinous or Apuleius.

If this be so, it can be seen as the tip of a rather large iceberg. First of all, in order to make appeal to the works of Plato, one needed to have a definitive edition of them. It was the suggestion long ago of Henri Alline[11] that the first edition of the works of Plato was instituted in the Academy under Xenocrates, and although this has been much impugned over the years as unprovable, I must say that it seems to me an entirely probable conjecture. Such an early edition was certainly made,[12] since we have what appears to be Plato's entire oeuvre surviving to us – something that cannot be claimed for any other ancient philosophic author, except perhaps Plotinus (and we know how *that* happened) – and I feel it to be unlikely that Speusippus ever got around to such an enterprise. It would most

---

[9] Actually, if Antiochus is following Xenocrates in this, Xenocrates' order will have been 'Ethics – Physics – Logic', and Sextus is merely following the preferred Stoic order.

[10] He might also have added that Aristotle seems to recognize a tripartition of philosophy at *Topics* 1.14 (105b19ff.).

[11] In Alline (1915).

[12] We must not, certainly, sweep under the carpet the unresolved problems attendant on the production of such a 'first edition'. For one thing, what order, or grouping, of the dialogues are we to imagine to have been adopted? And what would it mean to 'publish' such an edition? For some enlightening discussion of these problems, see Dorandi (2007). An intriguing straw in the wind is provided by a report by Antigonus of Carystus, writing in the mid-third century BCE (*ap.* Diog. Laert., *VP* 3.65), to the effect that 'when Plato's writings were first edited *with critical marks,* their possessors charged a certain fee for anyone who wished to consult them'. There is much that is obscure about this report, but at least it would seem to imply an earlier edition *without critical marks,* which certainly brings us back to the period of the Old Academy.

effectively underpin what seems to have been Xenocrates' main project, which is that of defending the tradition of Platonism against the attacks of Aristotle and his associates, such as Theophrastus, since to perform this duty plausibly he needed to have the Master's works to hand in a definitive format.

Once he had an authoritative corpus, he could proceed – though I think also that he had no hesitation in appealing to 'unwritten doctrines' when required, relying not only on his personal experience of what went on in the Academy, but on such a text as that from the *Seventh Letter* quoted above (if he did not actually compose that himself!). His purpose will have been to hammer out something like a coherent body of doctrine from this rather unpromising material.

If we take the sphere of ethics for a start, the sort of issues that were arising, in the wake of Aristotle's *Nicomachean Ethics* (in whatever form that might have been available), would have been the relative importance of the virtues and the lesser goods, those of the body and external circumstances, in the achieving of happiness, or *eudaimonia,* and the overall purpose of life, whether *theoria* or *praxis.*[13] From Plato himself, one might derive rather mixed signals, after all. From the *Phaedo,* for instance, one might conclude that the concerns of the body are simply a distraction for the philosopher, and should be unhitched from as far as possible, even before death (the philosopher should, precisely, practise death!), whereas from the *Republic,* particularly Book 9 (cf. esp. 580D–592B), one might deduce that the lesser goods, desired by the spirited element (*thymos*) and the passionate element (*epithymia*), though far inferior to the goods of the soul, are to be accorded a limited status, in a suitably controlled and moderated form. This ambiguity continues in the *Laws,* where, in Book 1, 631B–C, we learn that 'goods are of two kinds, human and divine; and the human goods are dependent on the divine, and he who receives the greater acquires also the less, or else he is bereft of both'. These 'human' goods, such as health, beauty, strength and wealth, Plato goes on to say, are far inferior to the 'divine' goods of the soul, which are the four virtues, but they are not to be dismissed from

---

[13] For an authoritative discussion of Plato's tripartition of goods, and the uses to which it was put in the later tradition, see Inwood (2014).

consideration. He goes on to characterize them, however, somewhat later (2, 661A–D), as 'conditional goods', which are really good only for the virtuous man, and actually evils for the bad man, who will be liable to misuse them.[14]

In face of all this, let us consider the definitions of happiness put forth by Xenocrates and Polemon respectively, as relayed to us by the Alexandrian Church Father Clement (*Strom.* 2.22). First that of Xenocrates, presumably derived from his treatise *On Happiness*:

> Xenocrates of Chalcedon defines happiness as the acquisition of the excellence (or virtue, *aretê*) proper to us, and of the resources with which to service it. Then as regards the proper seat (*to en hôi*) of this, he plainly says the soul; as the motive causes of it (*hyph' hôn*) he identifies the virtues; as the material causes (*ex hôn*), in the sense of parts, noble actions and good habits and attitudes (*hexeis kai diatheseis*); and as indispensable accompaniments (*hôn ouk aneu*), bodily and external goods.

There is much of interest here, if we can trust the basic fidelity of Clement. First of all, can we conclude from this that the distinctive 'metaphysic of prepositions', presumed by such an authority as Willy Theiler to be a product of the scholasticism of the first century BCE or later, is already being utilized by Xenocrates at the end of the fourth century? I'm not sure why not, really.[15] There is nothing inherent in the formulation, I think, that could not have been derived by a scholastically minded man from the existing, somewhat less systematic usage of prepositions for this purpose by Plato and Aristotle, and I am not sure how or why Clement would have arrived at this application of the prepositional terms, had he not had some stimulus to it from Xenocrates.

More important, however, is the content of the doctrine. We can deduce from this, I think, that *eudaimonia* is for Xenocrates not solely a matter of the acquisition or possession of *aretê*, but 'the resources with which to service it', that is to say, the bodily and

---

[14] This topic has been discussed, in exhaustive, and indeed rather exhausting, detail, by Bobonich (2002), in Chapter 2 of his vast work.

[15] I am conscious here of contradicting my earlier position in (2003), p. 141, where I assumed that such a formulation must be late Hellenistic; I can no longer see any compelling reason for this.

external goods which are its *hôn ouk aneu,* which I have rendered its 'indispensable accompaniments'.[16]

This in turn may be connected with evidence that can be derived from Cicero in *De Finibus* 4.15–18, where, in confutation of the Stoics, he is presenting the Antiochian view of the doctrine of the Old Academy and Peripatos, or more specifically, of Xenocrates and Aristotle. After declaring that these two start out from the same ethical first principles as do the Stoics later, the 'first things according to nature', or *prôta kata physin* (*prima naturae,* in Cicero's Latin), he proceeds to give a summary of their position. As this account does not accord particularly well with Aristotle's surviving views (though it may have accorded better with early works of his available to Cicero, but not to us), it seems reasonable to claim it, broadly, for Xenocrates:[17]

> Every natural organism aims at being its own preserver, so as to secure its safety and also its preservation true to its specific type.[18] With this object, they declare, man has called in the aid of the arts to assist nature; and chief among them is counted the art of living, which helps him to guard the gifts that nature has bestowed and to obtain those that are lacking. They further divided the nature of man into soul and body. Each of these parts they pronounced to be desirable for its own sake, and consequently they said that the virtues (or excellences) also of each were desirable for their own sakes; at the same time they extolled the soul as infinitely surpassing the body in worth, and accordingly placed the virtues also of the mind above the goods of the body. But they held that wisdom is the guardian and protectress of the whole man, as being the comrade and helper of nature, and so they said that the function of wisdom, as protecting a being that consisted of a mind and body, was to assist and preserve him in respect of both.

The principle with which this passage begins does not, admittedly, seem to reflect closely anything appearing in the Platonic dialogues;

[16] The issue of the role of the *hexeis kai diatheseis* as the 'parts' out of which happiness is constructed is also of interest, as it seems to embody a doctrine, also expressed by Aristotle at the beginning of Book 2 of the *Nicomachean Ethics* (1, 1103a14–b25), that *ethical* virtue arises from *ethos,* from good training and from the *practice* of noble deeds.
   On the fate of Plato's tripartition of goods and the uses to which it was put, see now Inwood (2014).
[17] I borrow the Loeb translation of H. Rackham, *Cicero De Oratore* (Cambridge, MA, 1969).
[18] *Omnis natura vult esse conservatrix sui, ut et salva sit et in genere conservetur suo.*

but it could well be a development of a principle enunciated by Plato's companion Eudoxus of Cnidus, who was noted for maintaining that pleasure was the highest good, on the grounds that the maximization of pleasure was the first thing sought by any sentient organism from its birth on.[19] If so, Xenocrates has adapted it to a rather different purpose, to establish a justification for maintaining a concern for physical survival and comfort as a base on which to build. On the other hand, the sentiments expressed in the rest of the text are readily derivable from the passages of the *Laws* mentioned above.

The establishing of 'the things primary according to Nature' as the basis for an ethical theory is attributed by Antiochus also to Polemon (e.g. *De Fin.* 4.50–1), but we may discern from reports of his position a slight increase in austerity, in comparison with his master Xenocrates. It can only have been slight, as they are consistently lumped together in the doxography, but it is significant that Polemon was the teacher of the future Stoic founder Zeno, and he plainly transmitted to him an austere ethical stance, which Zeno then developed further.

Clement reports Polemon's position, immediately following that of Xenocrates (*Strom.* 2.22):

> Polemon, the associate of Xenocrates, seems to wish happiness (*eudaimonia*) to consist in self-sufficiency (*autarkeia*) in respect of all good things, or at least the most and greatest of them. For he lays it down that happiness can never be achieved apart from virtue, *while virtue is sufficient for happiness even if bereft of bodily and external goods.*

It is in this last specification, if in anything, that Polemon is distinctive. One can see here, I think, traces of an on-going argument within the Academy as to the precise status of the so-called mortal goods. Nevertheless, it would seem from Antiochus' evidence that Polemon did not entirely dismiss these lower goods. Here is the passage alluded to above (4.50–1). Cicero is in the process of criticizing Cato for indulging in various specious Stoic arguments:

---

[19] Cf. Aristotle *Eth. Nic.* 1.12, 1101b27–31; 10.2, 1172b9–18. Aristotle remarks, in the second passage, that Eudoxus' views gained considerably in credibility because of his own high personal standards of morality. The basis for this principle might also perhaps be discerned in Diotima's 'basic law', enunciated at *Symp.* 207D, to the effect that 'the mortal does all it can to put on immortality', since this inevitably involves a desire for self-preservation.

> As for your other argument, it is by no means 'consequential', but actually dull-witted to a degree – though, of course the Stoics, and not you yourself, are responsible for that. Happiness is a thing to be proud of; but it cannot be the case that anyone should have good reason to be proud without virtue. The former proposition Polemon will concede to Zeno, and so will his Master (sc. Xenocrates) and the whole of their school, as well as all the other philosophers who, while ranking virtue far above all else, yet couple some other thing with it in defining the highest good; since if virtue is a thing to be proud of, as it is, and excels everything else to a degree hardly to be expressed in words, Polemon will be able to be happy if endowed solely with virtue, and destitute of all besides, and yet he will not grant you that nothing except virtue is to be reckoned as a good.

We have here, then, the lineaments of a Platonist doctrine on the first principles of ethics and the components of happiness, which, while allowing for variations of emphasis, yet can form the basis for a coherent position. In later times, it rather depended on whether you were more concerned to combat Stoics (as, for example, was Plutarch) or Peripatetics (as was the later Athenian Platonist Atticus) that you took a more or less austere line in ethics – that you favoured, for example, *metriopatheia* over *apatheia* or the reverse – but in either case there was a deposit of Platonist doctrine to fall back on, and that doctrine, I would maintain, was laid down by Xenocrates and Polemon, not immediately by Plato.

The case is similar in the area of the first principles of physics. Plato had left a rather confusing legacy to his successors – or so it must seem to us. We have, on the one hand, the Good of the *Republic*, a first principle which is in some way 'beyond' (*epekeina*) the rest of existence, of which it is the generative ground, as well as an object of desire; but then there is the Demiurge of the *Timaeus*, who is described as an Intellect, but who is represented as contemplating a Model in some way above and beyond himself, in his creation of Soul and of the world (unless the Demiurge and his creation are a myth, and to be deconstructed, as was stoutly maintained, against the criticisms of Aristotle, by both Speusippus and Xenocrates); then there is the One of the hypotheses of the second part of the *Parmenides*, which may or may not have been intended by Plato as a first principle, but which was certainly taken as such in later times;

further, there are the first principles set out in the *Philebus* (26Cff.), Limit, the Unlimited, and the Cause of the Mixture, which seem to have a fairly close relationship to the One and Indefinite Dyad of the Unwritten Doctrines; and then, last but not least, we seem to have the doctrine, firmly enunciated first in the *Phaedrus* (245Cff.), but also dominant in Book 10 of the *Laws*, of a rational World-Soul as the first principle of all motion, and therefore of all creation. What are we to do with this embarrassment of riches?

It is fairly plain what Xenocrates did with it; it is less plain in the case of Polemon, but I think that his position is recoverable, if certain minimal clues are probed closely. In either case, the result is interesting. In the case of Xenocrates, what is attested (though only by the doxographer Aetius, who is a rather doubtful witness)[20] is a pair of Monad and Dyad, the former being characterized as 'Zeus and Odd and Intellect', and spoken of in addition as 'having the role of Father, reigning in the heavens' – which latter description seems to connect him, remarkably, with the Zeus of the *Phaedrus* Myth (246E), and to place him, not in any transcendent relation to the physical cosmos, but rather as resident in the topmost sphere of it. In respect of his consort, however, there is what seems to me a serious difficulty in the text, which I have had various stabs at solving over the years, but which still bothers me. Here is the text as it appears in the *Placita:*

> Xenocrates, son of Agathenor, of Chalcedon [holds] as gods the Monad and the Dyad, the former as male, having the role of Father, reigning in the heavens (*en ouranôi basileuousan*), which he terms 'Zeus' and 'odd' (*perittos,* sc. numerically) and 'Intellect', which is for him the primary god; the other as female, in the manner of the Mother of the Gods (*mêtros theôn dikên*), ruling over the realm below the heavens, who is for him the Soul of the Universe (*psychê tou pantos*).

Here, on the face of it, it seems that the female principle which is the counterpart of the Monad, while being characterized as 'the mother of the gods', is also presented as a World-Soul, whose realm of operations is 'below the heavens'. Now I am on record as declaring that either Aetius has gone seriously astray here, or the manuscript

---

[20] *Placita,* 1.7, 30, p. 304 Diels = Fr. 15 Heinze/213 Isnardi Parente.

tradition has suffered corruption.[21] My reason for maintaining that is that we learn also, from the rather more reliable source that is Plutarch (*Proc. An.* 1012D–1013B = Fr. 68 H/188 IP), that, when Xenocrates is interpreting the creation of the soul in the *Timaeus* (35A–B), he takes the 'indivisible substance' (*ameristos ousia*) as being in fact the Monad, and 'that which is divided about bodies' (*hê peri ta sômata meristê*) as Multiplicity (*plêthos*),[22] or the Indefinite Dyad, while the Soul, characterized as a 'self-moving number' is the product of these two. So the Indefinite Dyad cannot itself be the World-Soul.

I would like to think that what has happened is that a line has fallen out of the Aetius passage, between *metros theôn* and *dikên,* in which we learned that the Dyad was female, 'holding the rank of Mother of the Gods, which he terms "Rhea" and "even" and "Matter"', while *dikên* actually is to be taken as a proper name, Dikê – the assessor of Zeus in Hesiod's *Works and Days* (256–7), and his 'follower' in *Laws* 4, 716A – characterizing the World-Soul as the offspring of these two entities, rather like Athene (who may also have been mentioned). This would, at any rate, provide us with a coherent account of Xenocrates' system of first principles, which in turn can be seen as an attempt to bring some order into the Platonic *testimonia.*

If we can take this as being the position, we can see, I think, Xenocrates going to work to create a coherent Platonist doctrine to counter the attacks of Aristotle (particularly in the *De Caelo* 1.12). An important part of his strategy is insisting on a non-literal interpretation of the *Timaeus,* since a literal interpretation creates various major embarrassments, which indeed Aristotle picked on. The first problem is the inconsistency of postulating something, to wit, the physical cosmos, that has a beginning but (by arbitrary decree of the Demiurge) no end. That is a logical absurdity, but there is also the difficulty of the Demiurge, though he appears to be a supreme deity, nonetheless contemplating a *paradeigma,* or 'model', in accordance with which he performs his creative work, which is apparently independent of, and co-ordinate with, himself; and there is also the oddity (though it is explained away by ingenious feats of modern

---

[21] Dillon (1983) (repr. (1990)). I have set out my arguments at more length in (2003), pp. 98–107.

[22] This is actually Speusippus' preferred term for the female principle, but Xenocrates doubtless employed it as well.

exegesis) that, although Timaeus has stated that an intellect cannot be present in anything without a soul (30b2–3), the Demiurge is precisely that – an intellect without a soul.[23]

However, once one has postulated that the account of demiurgic creation is a myth, all these problems dissolve satisfactorily. What the Demiurge then becomes, it seems to me, is nothing other than a divine Intellect, contemplating its own contents, which are the totality of the Forms, conceived by this stage as numbers, or at least numerical formulae of some sort, and projecting them, eternally, onto a substratum – which Plato himself, notoriously, does not present as matter, but which Aristotle, and very probably both Speusippus and Xenocrates also, did. This is also the Zeus of the *Phaedrus* myth, and perhaps also the Good of the *Republic*.

What, however, of the World-Soul of *Laws* 10, which would seem to be Plato's last word on the subject of supreme principles? It is not entirely clear to me what is going on here, and I am not sure that Polemon may not have had a slightly different take on it from Xenocrates, but I would suggest that, for Plato in the *Laws,* the supreme principles are indeed still the One and the Indefinite Dyad, but that they are seen as somehow, when considered separately, only *potential* principles, which must come together to be actualized, and the result of their coming together is the generation, first of the whole system of Form-Numbers, and then, with the addition of the principle of mobility and motivity, of Soul. Since this whole process must be conceived of as being eternal, and indeed timeless, the actively cosmogonic principle, and the cause of motion to everything else, is in fact the World-Soul.

At any rate, that is one version of a system of first principles that is bequeathed to later generations of Platonists, in the form of the triad of God – Forms, or even Form (*Idea*) – Matter, and this goes back, I suggest, primarily to Xenocrates, who, however, was assiduous in fathering it on Plato, and was able to quote a number of proof texts in support of this. That is not, however, the only system that emerges

---

[23] The ingenuity I refer to is to make a distinction between *having* an intellect, which would require something to have a soul, and *being* an intellect, which need not involve having or being anything else. That is all well and good, but, in the myth, the Demiurge is more than just a disembodied intellect; he is presented as a divine personage who *has* an intellect, and thus must also have a soul.

from the Old Academy, and this brings me back to Polemon, and to David Sedley.

We had long had the problem, and it was one that bothered me when I was surveying the Old Academy in the first chapter of *The Middle Platonists,* and for a long time after that, that, although Polemon presided over the Academy for nearly forty years, and was a deeply respected figure, all we seemed to know of him, apart from a cluster of anecdotes and sayings, was a modicum of ethical theory; he did not seem to have had any views on physics or logic at all. And yet could that be true? How could one profess to be a Platonist, after all, and disregard the whole metaphysical structure that underlay Plato's ethical theories? Certainly, Antiochus' spokesman Varro, in a passage of Cicero's *Academica* 1.24–9, gives us what purports to be a survey of Old Academic physics, but it comes across as so palpably Stoic in content that no one gave it a second thought.

However, one small clue does exist to Polemon's doctrine in this area which, if properly pressed, can yield interesting results, and it was this that Sedley fastened on in his article 'The Origins of Stoic God'. Immediately following on Aetius' rather extensive report of Xenocrates' theology, he appends a single line: 'Polemon declared that the cosmos is God (*Polemôn ton kosmon theon apephênato*).'

There were some who noted this doxographic snippet without finding it very interesting, as they felt that it could be rendered, 'Polemon declared that the cosmos is *a god*' – which would be a fairly uninteresting piece of information. But, in the context, it cannot mean that; Aetius is presenting various philosophers' views about the supreme deity, not about any old god. So we are faced with the testimony, albeit baldly doxographic, that, for Polemon, Platonist though he was, the supreme principle is none other than the cosmos. How can that be so?

We must first of all, I suggest, think back to Plato's last thoughts on the subject in *Laws* 10 – and, more particularly, to his faithful amanuensis Philip of Opus' appendix to that work, the *Epinomis*.[24] Philip, in the *Epinomis* (e.g. 976Dff.; 981B–E), comes out unequivocally in support of the position that the supreme principle is

---

[24] I must say that I am entirely convinced by the arguments of Leonardo Tarán in his fine edition of this work (1975) that this work is by Philip.

a rational World-Soul immanent in the cosmos, and indeed that the study of astronomy (rather than dialectic) is the highest science, since one is in fact thereby studying the motions of the divine mind. Philip had presumably convinced himself that this was indeed Plato's final view on the question, but he is actually presenting a rather radical take on Plato's thought, which was plainly not shared by his colleagues Speusippus or Xenocrates. Polemon, however, I would suggest, may have been attracted by it. But if indeed one adopts this view of the active first principle, what follows for one's doctrine of the dynamic structure of the cosmos as a whole? Let us consider Antiochus' account of the Old Academy's physical theory:

> The topic of Nature, which they treated next (sc. after ethics), they approached by dividing it into two principles, the one the creative (*efficiens* = *poiêtikê*), the other at this one's disposal, as it were, out of which something might be created. In the creative one they considered that there inhered power (*vis* = *dynamis*), in the one acted upon, a sort of 'matter' (*materia* = *hyle*); yet they held that each of the two inhered in the other, for neither would matter have been able to cohere if it were not held together by any power, nor yet would power without some matter (for nothing exists without being necessarily somewhere).[25] But that which was the product of both they called 'body' (*corpus* = *sôma*), and, so to speak, a sort of 'quality' (*qualitas* = *poiotês*).

What we have here is a two-principle universe admittedly very similar to that of the Stoics – but it is also, interestingly, similar to that attributed to Plato himself by Theophrastus in his curious little work, the *Metaphysics* (6a24–5). These two principles can, after all, be taken as the One and the Indefinite Dyad, or Limit and the Unlimited, neither of which can exist without the other, and the union of which generates, first Number and Soul, but ultimately the cosmos. Even the denominating of the active principle as a *dynamis,* and the formal principle (for that is what is being referred to) as *poiotês,* could be seen as deriving from a scholastic exegesis of the *Theaetetus,* first of 156A, where Socrates refers to active and passive principles in the cosmos as *dynameis,* and then to 182A, where he appears to coin the term *poiotês.*

---

[25] An interesting reference, this, to a passage of the *Timaeus,* 52B: 'Everything that exists must necessarily be in some place (*en tini topôi*).'

So even if we are driven to admit that Antiochus is giving something of a Stoic gloss to the material here, it seems reasonable to argue that he cannot have done so without some warrant from the Old Academic sources available to him.

A little further on, in ss. 27–8, the active principle is identified as a rational World-Soul, residing primarily in the heavens, but pervading all parts of the cosmos (it is in this sense that the cosmos as a whole can be described as God). It is 'perfect intelligence and wisdom (*mens sapientiaque perfecta*), which they call God, and is a sort of providence, presiding over all things that fall under its control'. There is nothing here, I think, that cannot be derived from a non-literal interpretation of the *Timaeus*.

We can see, then, I think, as in the case of ethical theory, something of a difference of emphasis between the doctrinal positions of Xenocrates and Polemon, though without constituting anything like a contradiction. The first beneficiaries of Polemon's doctrinal stance were the Stoics, but he then became available to such later figures as Eudorus of Alexandria, Nero's court philosopher Thrasyllus, and even the Platonizing Jewish philosopher Philo, all of whom adopted a rather Stoicizing logos-theology; while other philosophers, such as Plutarch and Atticus, will have been more influenced by Xenocrates. Between the two of them, however, they provided the basis for a body of Platonist dogma, extending from the first century BCE through the first two centuries CE.

I will pass lightly over the topic of logical theory and epistemology, since really most later Platonists adopted as Platonic the whole Aristotelian system of logic, together with such innovations as were added by Theophrastus and his successors. The Old Academic system of division of all things into categories of Absolute and Relative was not entirely forgotten but relegated rather to the background. The section of the *Academica* (1.30–2) devoted to logic, though, is not without interest, and indicates that Polemon was not oblivious to that either.

We may now pass on to consider a series of more detailed issues in the areas of ethics, physics and epistemology, but I hope that enough has been said here to make my main point, which is that the exigencies of inter-school rivalry, initially between the Academy and the Peripatos, but then between later Platonists and both Stoics and Aristotelians, demanded that Platonism become more formalized than it was left by Plato himself, and that it was primarily Xenocrates, in a vast array of treatises, both general and particular, who provided the bones of this organized corpus of doctrine. Not that the Platonists were ever subject to anything like a monolithic orthodoxy. Platonic doctrine was not anything handed down centrally, from above; it was rather a self-regulating system, in which everyone knew what it meant, broadly, to be a Platonist (which could, in later times, embrace being a Pythagorean as well), and managed to stay within those parameters, while squabbling vigorously with each other, as well as with the other schools, on various matters of detail.

CHAPTER 2

Monist and Dualist Tendencies in Platonism before Plotinus

We may begin our detailed investigations with a topic which goes to the heart of the Platonist project, and that is the question as to whether monism or dualism – in the moral sense, rather than in the metaphysical sense[1] – is the guiding principle which Plato bequeathed to his followers.

Plutarch of Chaeroneia, as he looked back at the legacy of his master Plato, had no doubt that Plato, having as he did a vivid sense of the power of evil in the world, was a dualist. In his most important surviving philosophical treatise, *On the Creation of the Soul in the Timaeus (De Proc. An.)*, he argues vigorously for Plato's postulation in that dialogue of a pre-cosmic disorderly soul which is ultimately responsible for the imperfections in the universe, despite being brought to a measure of order by the Demiurge, and he connects this up with a number of other key passages which seem to him to bear witness to the same sort of entity, such as *Theaetetus* 176A, where we are told that evil is endemic in this sphere of existence;[2] *Rep.* 2, 379C, where Socrates lays it down that God cannot be responsible for more than a small proportion of what happens to us;[3] *Politicus* 273B–D, where, in the context of the myth of the two world cycles, mention is made of the world's 'previous state' (*emprosthen hexis*) and

[1] That is to say, a dualism of good and evil principles, as opposed to a dualism of intelligible and sensible reality. Plato is certainly a dualist in the latter sense.

[2] 'Evil cannot be eliminated, Theodorus; there must always be some force ranged against Good.'

[3] 'Then God, being good, cannot be responsible for everything, as it is commonly said, but only for a small part of human life, for the greater part of which he has no responsibility. For we have a far smaller share of good than of evil, and while we can attribute the good to God, we must find something else to account for the evil.'

'ancient disharmony' (*palaia anharmostia*), which is always ready to reassert itself; and, last but not least, *Laws* 10, 896D–898C, where indeed we find a most interesting, and not a little troubling, postulate that the world is ruled not just by one, good soul, but by another as well, 'of the opposite capacity' (*tês tanantia dynamenês exergazesthai*). This last passage in particular has led to much discussion,[4] but it seems fair to say that the modern scholarly consensus, following Cherniss, is that, despite appearances, Plato does not intend to postulate a 'maleficent' soul (*kakergetis psyche*) as any sort of positive evil force in the world antithetical to God on the cosmic level. But if not, then what on earth, one may well ask, does he mean, both in this and the other passages mentioned?

In order to get a clearer perspective on this, we need, I think, to bring into the discussion Plato's system of first principles, according to accounts of the so-called Unwritten Doctrines: the One and the Indefinite Dyad.[5] The Dyad – or as Plato may indeed have termed it on occasion, the 'Great-and-Small' – is certainly in a sense antithetical to the One, but it is not to be viewed as in any way a positively evil principle. It is to be seen, rather, as simply the condition of there being a world at all – anything at all other than the absolute and barren simplicity of the One. Whether or not the temporal creation of the world by the Demiurge is to be taken literally (and I think that it is not)[6], the role of the Receptacle, though portrayed by Plato at *Tim.* 30A, and later at 52E–53A, as a source of disorderly motion, is really no more than the minimum postulate necessary to explain the diversity of a cosmos worthy of the name, that is, a system exhibiting the whole spectrum of possible varieties of being – even if some of them are not convenient to us, and therefore 'evil'.[7] The same opposition may be seen as being envisaged also in the other passages

---

[4] E.g. Cherniss (1954), pp. 23ff.; Görgemanns (1960), pp. 193–207; Halfwassen (2012) provides an excellent overview of the question, from the perspective of the so-called 'Tübingen School'.

[5] In fact, however, once one recognizes that these are indeed Plato's first principles (however mischievously presented by Aristotle at *Metaph.* A 6, 927a29ff., and elsewhere), it is not difficult to discern them as lying behind the Limit and Unlimitedness of *Philebus* 26Aff., as well as being alluded to at *Tim.* 48C and 53D.

[6] I have defended this position on a number of occasions, but cf. in particular Dillon, (1997a), repr. in Dillon (2012).

[7] See my remarks in the Introduction, p. 3.

mentioned, even in that in *Laws* 10 – the soul 'of the opposite tendency' need only be the element in the world that is responsible for multiplicity and diversity.

A confirmation of the essential monism of Plato's position comes to us, it seems to me, from the testimony of his follower Hermodorus of Syracuse, relayed by Simplicius, via Porphyry and Dercyllides (*In Phys.* p. 247, 30ff. = Hermodorus, Fr. 7 Isnardi Parente), where he declares, at the end of an extended account of Plato's first principles, that 'Matter (with which he identifies the Indefinite Dyad) is not a principle; and that is why it is said by Plato and his followers (*hoi peri Platona*) that there is only a single first principle.'

It is certainly in this sort of way that the opposition between the two principles is understood by Plato's nephew and successor Speusippus. He terms his two first principles One and Multiplicity (*plethos*), and presents the relationship between them as follows:[8]

> [O]ne must postulate two primary and highest principles, the One – which one should not even call existent (*on*), by reason of its simplicity and its position as principle of everything else, a principle being properly not yet that of which it is a principle – and another principle, that of Multiplicity, which is able of itself to facilitate division (*diairesin parekhesthai*) and which, if we are able to describe its nature most suitably, we would liken to a completely fluid and pliable matter. (*ap.* Iambl. *De Communi Mathematica Scientia* 4, p. 15, 5ff. Festa)

We may note that Speusippus presents Multiplicity here, not really as an active principle in opposition to the One, but rather as cooperating with the One in producing 'division', by which we must understand the diversity and individuation of the world – something that the One could not do by itself. As such, it is a partner rather than an opponent of the One. Indeed, in what follows Speusippus is concerned to deny the One the epithet 'good' (as a 'correction' of the position of his uncle Plato), as that would necessitate characterizing Multiplicity as 'evil', which it is not – how, he asks, would something intrinsically evil want to act against its own interests, and indeed in favour of its own dissolution, by helping to create something essentially good, i.e. the world?

---

[8] Following Philip Merlan (1960), I take the contents of ch. 4 of Iamblichus' *De Communi Mathematica Scientia* as substantially Speusippan, for reasons I have set out in Dillon (1984); see also Dillon (2003), pp. 40–6. This position is also taken up by Halfwassen, and by H.-J. Krämer before him.

This line of thought is manifested again in another interesting passage from Speusippus preserved by Proclus in his *Parmenides Commentary* (Book 7, pp. 38, 32–40 Klibansky), where, in some unknown context, Speusippus seems to be giving an 'ontological' interpretation of the first two hypotheses of Plato's *Parmenides,* according to which what is being portrayed in the second hypothesis is nothing other than the interaction between the One and the Indefinite Dyad, or Multiplicity, which is necessary for the generation of a world of individual beings. Proclus purports to quote him as follows (Speusippus is here attributing his doctrine, for strategic reasons, to the Pythagoreans):

> For they (sc. the Pythagoreans) held that the One is higher than Being and is the source of Being; and they delivered it even from the status of a principle. For they held that, given the One, in itself, conceived as separated and alone, without other things,[9] with no additional element, nothing else would come into existence. And so they introduced the Indefinite Dyad as the principle of beings.

What the Indefinite Dyad contributes, of course, is a process of division, leading initially to the generation of the series of natural numbers, as set out in *Prm.* 143A–144A, but ultimately of everything else. Thus, for Speusippus, there are indeed two principles in the universe, but they are not opposed to one another; the second, or 'material'[10] one offers itself to the first as the facilitator of division and individuation, in order to bring a world into being. If the two principles are to be regarded as opposed at all, it is rather as active to passive – though the 'passive' principle yet serves as the facilitator of an essential cosmic process.

Speusippus, then, comes across as a pretty unequivocal monist.[11] With Xenocrates, on the other hand, we might be forgiven for discerning

---

[9] This phrase may indeed be an intentional reminiscence of *Prm.* 143a6–8: 'Now take just this "One" which we are saying has being, and conceive it just by itself alone, apart from the being which we say it has.' If this be accepted, it would support my contention that Speusippus is actually engaged on an exegesis of the second hypothesis.

[10] The use of the term *hyle* to characterize Multiplicity in the earlier passage from Iamblichus has raised some eyebrows, as the first use of the word in its technical sense is normally attributed to Aristotle (as opposed to Plato); but we do not need to suppose that Aristotle was the exclusive initiator of this terminology – and even if he was, there is no reason to deny that his older contemporary Speusippus could not have borrowed it. The term is actually being used here rather tentatively.

[11] On the subject of evil, we may note, at the end of the *DCMS* 4 passage (p. 18, 9–12 Festa), that Speusippus is reported as declaring that there is nothing either ugly or bad (*aiskhron*

certain tendencies to dualism. He, like his predecessors, adopts a pair of first principles, the Monad and the Indefinite Dyad,[12] who between them generate, first, Number, then Soul, and then the rest of creation, very much in the manner of Speusippus (though no doubt with variations that would be clearer to us if we had more, or indeed any, of their respective works), so that on that level he is no more dualist than they are; but he exhibits other features that seem to reveal some tendency to dualism at a lower level – a sort of modified dualism.

What we learn, chiefly from Plutarch,[13] but also from elsewhere,[14] is that Xenocrates, in the course of making an interesting three-way division of the universe, places the sublunar realm under the rule of a 'lower Zeus', who is also to be identified as Hades. This Hades may be a far cry from a Gnostic-style ignorant or wicked Demiurge, but he may on the other hand have some connection with an entity that Plutarch produces in the essay *On the E in Delphi* (393B–C), and identifies with Pluto/Hades, who rules the sublunar realm. This figure, which is contrasted with a transcendent deity, identified here, not with Zeus, but with Apollo,[15] presides over the changeableness of our world, and regulates it in the interests of the higher deity. They are contrasted, then,[16] but not radically opposed. What we have here, rather, is a contrast between a primary and a secondary deity, the latter being immediately responsible for the multiplicity, changeability, and illusoriness characteristic of the physical, sublunar world.

---

oude kakon) in the higher reaches of reality – the realm of the One, of Number, or of Figure, 'but only at the lowest level, among the fourths and fifths, which are combined from the lowest elements, does evil come into being – and even then not principally (*proêgoumenôs*), but as a result of falling-away and failure to control what is in accordance with nature'. The 'fourths and fifths' are rather obscure categories, but are probably meant to represent animate and inanimate physical objects respectively. At any rate, here we have evil presented as very much an *incidental* product of the cosmic system.

[12] Cf. Fr. 15 Heinze/213 Isnardi Parente – a doxographic report from Aetius, which is not, unfortunately, without problems. See Dillon (1986).

[13] In *Platonic Questions* 9, 1007F = Fr. 18H/216IP.

[14] E.g. the Aetius fragment mentioned earlier, and Clement of Alexandria, *Strom.* 5.14 = Fr. 18H/217IP.

[15] For the sake of the word-play, '*a-polla*', 'not-many' – or perhaps in the more elaborate form presented much later by John Laurentius Lydus (*De Mens.* 2. 12) *apothen tôn pollôn* – highlighting the unitary nature of the supreme deity.

[16] As indicated by the epithets bestowed upon each – Apollo ('not-many'), Dêlios (interpreted as 'clear'), Phoibos ('bright'), and so on; while the lower divinity is Plouton (in the sense of 'abounding in wealth', and so in multiplicity and variety), Aidôneus ('unseen'), and Skotios ('dark').

It is interesting, finally, that, just a little earlier in the dialogue (388E–389B), Plutarch makes a similar contrast, but this time between Apollo and Dionysus – but we have to bear in mind that, at least as far back as Heraclitus (cf. Fr. B15 D–K), the figures of Hades and Dionysus are, in a curious way, linked. It must be admitted that the authority of Xenocrates is nowhere appealed to in this context, but the fact remains that he had originally set up the contrast between a supreme being and a secondary divinity, identified with Hades, who rules below the Moon.

At any rate, apart from this, Xenocrates also – again, according to Plutarch[17] – entertained the concept of evil or malevolent daemons, 'great and strong natures (*physeis*) in the atmosphere, malevolent and morose, who rejoice in gloomy sacrifices, and after gaining them as their lot, they turn to nothing worse'. These beings, in fact, constitute Xenocrates' explanation of the existence of unpleasant or obscene religious rituals, which he feels would be inappropriate to the goodness of God or the gods, but which serve to propitiate these evil forces in the universe.[18]

This seems a radical departure from Plato's concept of the daemonic nature, as set out, above all, in *Symp.* 202E, in the direction of some form of popular belief, but when tied in with Xenocrates' postulation of a 'lower Zeus' on the one hand, and a curious report in Damascius[19] that Xenocrates understood Socrates' reference at *Phd.* 62B to our being in mortal bodies as 'on a kind of guard-duty' as being a reference to our 'Titanic' nature, which 'culminates in Dionysus' (*eis Dionyson koryphoutai*), it takes on a deeper significance. This latter reference in Damascius is most obscure and compressed, but behind it there does seem to lurk a belief in an Orphic-style 'sinful' human nature, arising from, in mythical terms, our descent from the ashes of the Titans who devoured Dionysus. Allegorized and de-mythologized, this could be seen to identify Dionysus with Hades, or the 'lowest Zeus', as ruler of our sublunar world, and thus tie in with the passages from the *On the E at Delphi* discussed above. One seems here to get glimpses of dimensions to Xenocrates' thought-world of which we know very little, but which

[17] At *On Isis and Osiris* 361B.   [18] On this topic, see Schibli (1993).
[19] *In Phaedonem* I p. 85 Norvin = Fr. 20H/219IP.

point in the direction of at least a modified dualism. The notion that
our realm of existence is presided over by a divinity that is distinct
from, and even antithetical to, the supreme deity, is one that was to
have quite a lively future in the first few centuries CE.

This, I think, is the furthest extent to which dualism could be
imputed to the Old Academy.[20] The New Academy we may pass
over, as not believing much in anything, but when we come down to
the revived dogmatism of Antiochus of Ascalon in the first century
BCE, we find a very much Stoicized system, featuring an active
principle and a passive, material one (cf. the exposition of Platonist
philosophy by Antiochus' spokesman, Varro, in Cic. *Acad. Post.*
27ff.). Matter is a substance 'formless and devoid of all quality', so
that it is not in any position to offer any sort of resistance to the
operations of the active principle. We may not have the whole story
on Antiochus, of course, but there is certainly no sign of dualism in
what remains to us of him.

   The same may be said of Eudorus of Alexandria, in the next
generation, despite a strong infusion of Neopythagoreanism into
his philosophical position. However, Eudorus, while adopting the
pair of Monad and Indefinite Dyad, postulates a supreme One above
both of these, which forms an absolute ground of all existence, even
matter. Eudorus may here be drawing creatively on the system set out
in Plato's *Philebus* (26E–30E), where the Cause of the Mixture is
postulated over and above the pair of Limit and Unlimitedness, but
this innovation of his is clear indication of a monistic tendency.

Only when we reach Plutarch, in the late first century CE, do we find
an unequivocal onset of dualism. We have seen already his adoption,
and possible development, of the modified dualism of Xenocrates, but
that is only part of the story. Besides this subordinate sublunar deity,
Plutarch postulates a much more radically evil power in the universe.[21]

---

[20]   We know very little about the metaphysics of Polemon, the last head of the Old Academy,
      but, if I am right in supposing that it was primarily his synthesis of Platonic doctrine on
      which Antiochus of Ascalon is building later, we may conclude that there is not much sign
      of dualism in his thought, despite his loyalty to his master Xenocrates. See further my
      discussion of Polemon in Chapter 1, pp. 20–22 above.
[21]   I have discussed this topic more fully in Dillon (2002a).

This emerges, in mythological form, in his essay *On Isis and Osiris*, in the person of Typhon, or alternatively, in terms of Persian religion, Ahriman (Areimanios). There is an enlightening statement of his position at 369E:

> There has, therefore, come down from the theologians and lawgivers to both poets and philosophers[22] this ancient belief, which is of anonymous origin, but is given strong and tenacious evidence – that the universe is not kept on high of itself without mind and reason and guidance, nor is it only one principle that rules and directs it as it were by rudders and curbing reins, but that many powers do so who are a mixture of evil and good. Rather, since Nature, to be plain, contains nothing unmixed, it is not one steward that dispenses our affairs for us, as though mixing drinks from two jars in a hotel.[23] Life and the cosmos, on the contrary – if not the whole of the cosmos, at least the earthly one below the moon, which is heterogeneous, variegated and subject to all manner of changes[24] – are compounded of two opposite principles (*arkhai*) and of two antithetic powers (*dynameis*), one of which leads by a straight path and to the right, while the other reverses and bends back. For if nothing comes into being without a cause, and if good could not provide the cause of evil, then Nature must contain in itself the creation and origin of evil, as well as of good.

These two 'antithetic powers', structured rather like the two circles of the soul in the *Timaeus* (36B–D), are presented as constituting a sort of tension of opposites, by virtue of which the world is preserved in being. In the essay *On the Obsolescence of Oracles* (428Fff.), it is the Indefinite Dyad which takes on the role of the 'evil' principle, showing how differently it is viewed in Plutarch's thought from its role in that of Plato or Speusippus.

> Of the supreme principles, by which I mean the One and the Indefinite Dyad, the latter, being the element underlying all form-lessness and disorder, has been called Unlimitedness (*apeiria*); but the nature of the One limits and contains what is void and irrational and indeterminate in Unlimitedness, gives it shape, and renders it in some way tolerant and receptive of definition.

---

[22] He has just quoted Heraclitus and Euripides.

[23] This is a rather creative allusion to the Homeric image of the two jars standing in the hall of Zeus, out of which he dispenses good and evil to men (*Il.* 24.527–8).

[24] This may be a devious allusion to his other 'modified dualist' theory.

We note that it is 'the element underlying all formlessness and disorder'. Number, and the cosmos, is created by the One 'slicing off' greater or smaller sections of multiplicity (429A). 'If the One is done away with', says Plutarch, 'once more the Indefinite Dyad throws all into confusion, and makes it to be without rhythm, bound or measure.'

An aspect of the Dyad is the disorderly World-Soul which Plutarch discerns as animating the pre-cosmic state of things in the *Timaeus*, and which he equates with the 'maleficent' soul of *Laws* 10. Here is what he has to say in his essay *On the Generation of the Soul in the Timaeus* (1014B):

> For creation does not take place out of what does not exist at all but rather out of what is in an improper or unfulfilled state, as in the case of a house or a garment or a statue. For the state that things were in before the creation of the ordered world (*kosmos*) may be characterized as 'lack of order' (*akosmia*); and this lack of order was not something incorporeal or immobile or soulless, but rather it possessed a corporeal nature which was formless and inconstant, and a power of motion which was frantic and irrational. This was the disorderly state of a soul which did not yet possess reason (*logos*).

The disorderly element, then, which Plato in the *Timaeus* (48A, 56C, 68E) calls Necessity (*anankê*), cannot be taken as something simply negative and characterless, such as matter, but must be a positive force, the disorderly or 'maleficent' soul. Even this entity, however, is at least open to being brought to order by the Demiurge – and in the case of Isis in the *Isis and Osiris,* positively desirous of it. Behind this again, as I have said, there seems to lurk, in Plutarch's system, a more absolutely evil force, and here it is hard not to see some influence from Persian sources.

It would appear, after all, that there is a degree of dualism in the air of the second century CE. Later in the century, the Neopythagorean Numenius of Apamea is attested as propounding a relatively dualistic version of Pythagoreanism, as compared, say, to that set out in the account given by Alexander Polyhistor (*ap.* Diog. Laert. 8.24–33) in the first century BCE, in which the Dyad is produced as 'matter' for itself by the Monad, resulting in an essentially monistic system, which seems to represent the earlier strand of Pythagorean thinking.

Numenius' more immediate predecessors in the tradition, Moderatus of Gades and Nicomachus of Gerasa, do not show their hand very clearly on the matter of relations between Monad and Dyad, but, on the basis of what survives to us, appear to take a relatively monistic stance. Numenius, however, in his account of the nature of Matter, preserved to us by Calcidius,[25] comes across as firmly dualist. He identifies it with the Indefinite Dyad, and the Maleficent Soul as propounded by Plutarch, and actually criticizes those Pythagoreans (perhaps including Moderatus), who think that

> that indefinite and immeasurable Dyad was produced by the Monad withdrawing from its own nature and departing into the form of the Dyad – an absurd situation, that that which had no existence should come to subsist, and that thus Matter should come to be out of God, and out of unity immeasurable and limitless duality.

He goes on (lines 33ff.) to describe Matter as fluid and without quality, but yet a positively evil force, criticizing the Stoics for postulating it as 'indifferent, and of a median nature'. For Plato, he says, it is rather the compound of Form and Matter that has this quality, not Matter itself – and, like Plutarch, he appeals to Plato's doctrine in *Laws* 10.

This dualism that Numenius propounds holds equally well for the composition of the individual human being. Our lower, irrational soul derives from the evil, material Soul in the cosmos, and here Numenius plainly went further than other Platonists, in postulating in us a separate soul emanating from matter, with, presumably, its own set of 'evil' faculties. Porphyry, in reporting Numenius' distinctive doctrine,[26] does, admittedly, characterize this soul as 'irrational' (*alogos*), but he may be using this term somewhat loosely, by contrast with the rational soul descending from above. This second soul is a distinctively dualistic element in Numenius' thought, reminiscent of what St Paul talks of (e.g. Romans 7:23; 8:7–8) as 'the law of sin which dwells in my members' and wars against the spirit, a source of psychic energy which is not so much irrational as downright perverse. It also seems to relate to an interesting report of Origen's, in Book 3, ch. 4 of his treatise *On First Principles* (*De Principiis*), where he

[25] *In Tim.* chs. 295–9 = Fr. 52 Des Places.
[26] *On the Powers of the Soul*, Fr. 253 Smith = Fr. 44 Des Places.

discusses the postulate that we have within us, not just a Platonic tripartite or bipartite soul, but two distinct souls. The immediate target here seems to be Gnostics of some sort (since they quote Scripture – notably St Paul – to their purpose), but Origen also knew Numenius perfectly well, and probably has him in mind too. In any case, this seems to be here an instance of cross-fertilization between Numenius and the Gnostic tradition.

To sum up, then, the Platonism that Plotinus inherits – setting aside Ammonius Saccas, of whom we know all too little – is by the later second century distinctly dualist in tendency, and is able, especially in the case of Plutarch, to quote Plato to its purpose. Plato himself, though, I would maintain, is, despite appearances to the contrary, what one might term a 'modified monist'. That is to say, he fully recognizes the degree of imperfection and evil in the world, and holds it to be ineradicable, but he does not in the last resort believe in a positive countervailing force to the Good or the One.

What we have is simply a negative force, whether Indefinite Dyad, disorderly World-Soul, or Receptacle, which is an inevitable condition of there being a world at all, but which, as a side-effect of introducing diversity, generates various sorts of imperfection. It is this scenario that justifies his follower Hermodorus, as we have seen, in declaring that Plato recognizes only a single first principle, and it is to this sort of monism – if anything, in a more pronounced form – that Plotinus returns, reacting most immediately to the strong dualism of Numenius, but also to that of contemporary Gnostics – with whom, as we know, he had a certain amount of interaction.[27]

---

[27] His opposition to them culminates in his treatise 2.9 (33), *Against the Gnostics*, but he can be seen to take side-swipes at them elsewhere in his works. Further, Porphyry tells us in ch. 16 of his *Life of Plotinus* that Plotinus 'often attacked their position in his lectures'.

CHAPTER 3

The Ideas as Thoughts of God

The precise origin of the concept of the Platonic Forms, or Ideas, as thoughts of God is a long-standing puzzle in the history of Platonism, which I am on record as dismissing somewhat brusquely in various works.[1] I am glad to have an opportunity to return to it now, in the present context of a study of the development of Platonism as a philosophical system. I propose to begin my consideration of it by returning to the seminal article of Audrey Rich, published in *Mnemosyne* back in 1954.[2] Rich's thesis in that article was that the concept arose, whenever it arose – some time in the early Hellenistic age was her guess – as a reaction to Aristotle's concept of the Unmoved Mover of *Metaphysics* Lambda as an intellect thinking itself, and 'a desire to reconcile the Theory of Ideas with the Aristotelian doctrine of immanent form' (p. 132).

It seems to me that Rich was broadly correct in this conjecture, but that she was simply too cautious in her attribution of the origin of the theory. I would argue – and have indeed argued on a number of occasions before this – that really all that is required for the development of such a theory (though no doubt stimulated by both the theorizing and the gibes of Aristotle) is the postulation that the account of the nature and activities of the Demiurge in Plato's *Timaeus* is not to be taken literally; and we know this position to have been maintained, among his immediate successors, by both Speusippus and Xenocrates.[3] After all, once it has been agreed that the Demiurge and his temporal creative activities, involving his contemplating of a Paradigm distinct from, and logically superior

---

[1] E.g. Dillon (1977), p. 95; (2003), pp. 107–11.   [2] Rich (1954), pp. 123–33.
[3] Scholiast on Ar. *De Caelo* 279b32ff. = Speusippus, Fr. 61 Tarán.

to himself, is a myth, the alternative more or less imposes itself of a divine intellect eternally engaged in creative activity, modelling the physical universe which it creates upon a system of formal principles which constitute the contents of its intellect. How this would have worked for Speusippus is less perspicuous, I think, than how it would have worked for Xenocrates,[4] so it is to Xenocrates that I prefer to turn.

First of all, it seems best to distinguish what we know, or think we know, about Xenocrates' theology, before we turn to the airing of conjectures, however plausible. From the doxographic notice of Aetius (*Placita* 1.7, 30, p. 304 Diels[5] = Fr. 15 Heinze/213 Isnardi Parente), we may gather that, for Xenocrates, the supreme principle was, among other things, an Intellect. The relevant part of the passage runs as follows:

> Xenocrates, son of Agathenor, of Chalcedon, <holds> as gods the Monad and the Dyad, the former as male, having the role of Father, reigning in the heavens (*en ouranôi basileuousan*), which he terms Zeus and odd (*perittos*) and intellect (*nous*), which is for him the primary God.

We have, then, a primary God (*prôtos theos*), who is both unitary and an intellect (no contradiction between these two characterizations, it seems, being discerned by philosophers before Plotinus). The Monad is also identified by Xenocrates, as we learn from Plutarch (*Proc. An.* 1012E), as 'the undivided and unchanging' element in the formation of the World-Soul by the Demiurge at *Ti.* 35A. This latter piece of information might seem to pose a problem, but it really ceases to be such, if we bear in mind the other fact that we think we know about Xenocrates, mentioned above: to wit, that he did not take the creation account in the *Timaeus* literally. This would make it more or less inevitable that the Demiurge be identified with Xenocrates' Nous-Monad, and that it is the blending of this entity with his second principle, the Indefinite Dyad (represented by 'that substance which is divided about bodies'), that produces Soul.

---

[4] For Speusippus, after all, the supreme principles are a (supra-essential) One and an Indefinite Dyad, or (principle of) Multiplicity (*plêthos*), so that demiurgic activity proper, together with the generation of Forms (and their projection on the material substratum to form the physical world) becomes the role rather of the World-Soul.

[5] Originally derived from Stobaeus, *Anth.* 1, 36 Wachs.

If the above be accepted as data that we can rely on, then all that calls for conjecture, it seems to me, is the contents of this divine intellect. Here, although explicit evidence fails us, we are left with some pointers. We know a certain amount about Xenocrates' theory of Forms, after all, albeit mainly from the hostile reports of Aristotle. Aristotle reports indignantly (or derisively)[6] that Xenocrates identified the Forms with numbers, but he nowhere specifies where Xenocrates wished to situate them. From certain remarks of Theophrastus, however, in his little aporetic volume entitled *Metaphysics*[7] (2.10, 5b26ff.), we might conclude that some Platonist (presumably Xenocrates) had a concept of the first principle that combined Aristotle's Unmoved Mover (about which Theophrastus has just been raising some problems) with something rather more positive, derived from a demythologized interpretation of the *Timaeus*. The problem that Theophrastus is raising here is why, if the first principle wishes the best for all its products, they are not all equally good:[8]

> And if from the best comes the best, the heavenly bodies should derive something finer than their rotation from the first principle, unless indeed they were prevented by not being able to receive anything better; *for surely that which is first and most divine is something that wishes for everything what is best.* But perhaps this is something immoderate and not to be sought for; for he who says this is demanding that all things should be alike and in the best of all states, exhibiting little or no difference between them.

Now this may or may not be a very effective line of criticism. The important thing for our purposes, though, is what it is a criticism *of*. Not, surely, any longer Aristotle's Prime Mover, for that wishes nothing for anything. This entity seems rather to be a combination of the Aristotelian Prime Mover with something like a demythologized Timaean Demiurge, who does 'wish all things to be as good as possible' (*Ti.* 29E);[9] and that, I suggest, is the sort of entity that Xenocrates wished to postulate his Nous-Monad as being.

[6] E.g. *Metaph.* H 2, 1028b24ff.; M 1, 1076a20ff.; M 9, 1085a5ff.
[7] Or whatever its real name was: possibly *On First Principles*, or *On Basic Problems*.
[8] I have discussed this passage already in Dillon (2002b).
[9] I take the italicized portion of the text above to be a fairly explicit reminiscence of this passage of the *Timaeus*.

What we seem to have here, then, is a Prime Mover with some form of outward-directed intentionality; and it can hardly wish the best for all things without having some conception, first of all, of the things concerned, and secondly, what would be their best state. We have here, then, a God with thoughts, thoughts which are formative of physical reality.

To support this, there is also the contemporary, if rather dim-witted, attestation of the Sicilian Alcimus,[10] reported by Diogenes Laertius (*VP* 3.13), that 'each one of the Forms is eternal, a thought (*noēma*), and moreover impervious to change'. Alcimus does not specify who is thinking the thought that each Form is, but in the context it really cannot be an individual human mind; the Forms must be the thoughts of an eternal Thinker. Such a report need not be dismissed out of hand as a misunderstanding of Plato's own doctrine;[11] it may well reflect the accepted position of the Academy under Xenocrates.

Lastly, the Xenocratean definition of the soul – also satirized by Aristotle[12] – as 'number moving itself' (*arithmos heauton kinôn*) would seem to indicate that, since Forms are held by Xenocrates to be numbers, what Soul does is to set in motion, and project further, the Forms that are imprinted on it by Intellect. What Soul adds to what it receives from Intellect is *motion*, in the sense of both mobility and motivity.

The evidence, then, for the doctrine of Forms as thoughts of God in the Old Academy, at least from Xenocrates on, while no more than circumstantial, is, I think, reasonably plausible.[13] We must now examine the further stages of its development, where the evidence is firmer.

---

[10] Alcimus' purpose in writing his book was to prove that Plato had borrowed all his best ideas from Epicharmus – a piece of Sicilian chauvinism over which we will draw a veil.

[11] After all, the argument presented in the *Parmenides* (132Bff.) against the Forms being thoughts need not be relevant here. That is an argument against subjectivity: the Forms in this case being merely constructs of the human mind.

[12] *De An.* 1.2, 404b27–8, etc. (= Fr. 60 H/165-87 IP).

[13] While recognizing that we have no explicit evidence of Polemon's views on the Forms or their proper place, there is no reason to suppose that he would have dissented from the position of Xenocrates in this matter.

First we must turn to Antiochus of Ascalon. In March 2012 there appeared a distinguished collection of essays on Antiochus, products of a conference held in Cambridge in July 2007 (in which I was not involved),[14] and I have been interested by the attitudes of the participants to the possibility that Antiochus had a Theory of Forms of any kind. There is an 'austere' view of the evidence, propagated by Jonathan Barnes in an influential paper,[15] which basically denies that we can attribute to Antiochus anything like a Platonic Theory of Forms, and this line is broadly followed by, for instance, Charles Brittain, while Mauro Bonazzi, and, I am glad to say, David Sedley, adopt a more 'generous' interpretation of the evidence, with which I would concur. Neither, however, seems to me to accord proper attention to the evidence of Antiochus' faithful follower M. Terentius Varro, to which I would accord considerable weight (see below).

It was the view of Willy Theiler,[16] enunciated back in 1930, that the theory of the Forms as thoughts of God was in fact an innovation of Antiochus himself. As will be clear from what has preceded, I do not see this theory as Antiochus' invention, but I do agree that Antiochus contributes a new twist to it. This 'twist' comes, in my view, from Antiochus' thoroughgoing adoption of Stoic metaphysics. This in turn results from Antiochus' judgement that the Stoic doctrine of God and his relation to the world may be viewed as merely a formalization of Plato's doctrine in the *Timaeus,* as this was rationalized in the later Academy by Xenocrates and Polemon. This rationalization involves, first, demythologizing the account of the creation of the soul and the world by the Demiurge, so that the Demiurge becomes a divine intellect, whose action upon the universe is eternal rather than initiated at a point in time, and who is employing for this action, not any kind of 'paradigm' external to himself, but rather the contents of his own intellect. If Polemon contributed anything further to this scenario, it would in my view be the specification that this divine intellect is not transcendent over, but immanent within the cosmos – if we may derive that conclusion from the

---

[14] Sedley (ed.) (2012).
[15] 'Antiochus of Ascalon', in Griffin & Barnes (eds.) (1989), pp. 51–96 (see esp. Appendix E).
[16] Theiler (1930).

admittedly very bald doxographic report by Aetius[17] that 'Polemon declared that the cosmos was God', which I have discussed at more length above in Chapter 1.

This in turn brings us very near to the Stoic position, as enunciated by Polemon's erstwhile pupil Zeno of Kition. The only question that remains uncertain is whether Polemon still retained a belief in immaterial essence, as being proper to God – and indeed to Forms and Soul – or whether he had been prepared to entertain the theory that was going the rounds in some quarters in the later Academy (such as Heraclides of Pontus, for example)[18] that soul, at least, and possibly also the supreme divinity, was composed instead of a very special kind of fire (comparable to Aristotelian aether), of which the stars also are composed.

I put forward this possibility only very tentatively, and it is by no means crucial to my overall position. There is no need to deny Zeno and his followers a certain measure of originality, and the development of a doctrine of 'craftsmanly fire' (*pyr tekhnikon*) as a suitable material for the Active Principle of the universe to be composed of can be seen as a reasonable solution to certain worries about the mode of interaction between immaterial and material essence that seem to have been besetting the Academy in the decades before Zeno appeared on the scene. After all, a key dictum on this topic can be derived (and seems to have been so derived by Zeno, among others – including Antiochus later) from Plato's *Sophist* 248C: 'We proposed as a sufficient mark of real things the presence in a thing of the power of being acted upon or of acting in relation to however insignificant a thing.' The conclusion is ready to hand that things cannot act upon one another, or be acted upon, unless they have some quality or substance in common, and that would be some degree of materiality.

However, I am in danger of wandering from the main point. This is all by way of background to what I wish to maintain, to wit, that Antiochus need not have felt that accepting the Stoic doctrine of *pyr tekhnikon* or *pyr noeron* was in conflict with his position as

---

[17] Reported in Stobaeus, *Anth.* 1, 36, 5 W-H, just before his doxographic report of Xenocrates' views, discussed above. It is not in fact entirely clear to me whether Xenocrates in his turn regarded this supreme Nous-Monad as transcending the cosmos, as he presents it as 'ruling in the heavens'. But that cannot be pressed too far, I suppose.

[18] Cf. Frs. 98–9 Wehrli.

a champion of the Old Academy – an institution about whose views, as we must continually remind ourselves, he knew a great deal more than we do. Once that is accepted, it seems to me that Antiochus can both employ very Platonic-sounding terminology to describe the Forms, as he (or at least his spokesman, 'Varro') does at *Acad.* 1.30–2: 'that which is eternally simple and uniform and identical with itself' – a formulation borrowed pretty closely from *Phd.* 78D – and yet view these Forms, or this system of Forms, as none other than the system of *logoi spermatikoi* constituting the contents of the cosmic Logos, this Logos in turn being for him nothing other than an updating and rationalization of the Demiurge and World-Soul of the *Timaeus*. And of course, in the Stoic system, which Antiochus could quite happily adopt, the contents of the cosmic Logos are reflected in the contents of our individual minds, since our minds are mere sparks, so to speak, emanating from the cosmic Logos. In this way, the Forms can be also seen as concepts (*ennoiai* or *prolêpseis*) in our minds. This does not, however, make them purely subjective entities, as they are only reflections of the *logoi spermatikoi* in the Logos.

Now all this seems to me quite a logical development, and it appears perfectly reasonable also that Antiochus should express himself, in describing his Theory of Forms, with what must seem to us a certain degree of systematic ambiguity, but I have to recognize that, to a certain type of scholarly mind of the Barnesian persuasion, all this appears quite fantastic. To quote Barnes himself, in the paper above-mentioned: 'Any attempt to reconstruct Antiochus' thought requires fantasy and imagination. But fantasy must be responsible to the evidence, and imagination must acknowledge one sobering fact: we do not know very much about Antiochus.' My reply to that is that, if one is not prepared to make (judicious) use of fantasy and imagination, not only in respect of Antiochus, but also in respect of the Old Academy and of Middle Platonism in general, one had better steer clear of the area altogether. It all depends, after all, what one regards as 'evidence'; the attitude of a forensic defence lawyer, favoured by Barnes and others, such as Charles Brittain, is not going to get us very far at all.

That said, I turn to what I regard as a decisive piece of evidence as to Antiochus' theory of the Forms as thoughts of God, and that is a passage from the works of his follower Varro, preserved in Augustine's *De Civitate Dei* (7.28).[19] The context is slightly odd, but compelling enough for all that. I will quote it at some length, as it gives a useful insight into Varro's Antiochian theology in general:[20]

> What success attends the effort of Varro, that shrewdest of scholars, to reduce those gods, by would-be subtle arguments, to the sky and the earth, and give that reference to them all? The attempt is impossible. The gods wriggle out of his clutches; they jump from his hands, slip away, and tumble to the ground. Before speaking of the females, the goddesses that is, he says:
>
> 'As I have already said in the first book about places,[21] there are two recognized sources of origin for the gods, the sky and the earth. Hence some gods are called celestial, others terrestrial. I started, earlier on, with the sky, speaking about Janus, whom some have identified with the sky, others with the world. So now I will begin to treat of feminine deities by speaking about Tellus.'
>
> I understand the difficulty experienced by an intelligence of such range and quality. A plausible line of argument leads him to see the sky as an active principle, the earth as passive. And so he attributes masculine energy to the former, feminine to the latter; and he fails to realize that the activity in both spheres is the activity of him who created both.[22] Varro uses the same line of interpretation in his previous book,[23] in dealing with the celebrated mysteries of Samothrace.

---

[19] The suggestion, put forward by Barnesians (such as David Blank in the collection of essays above-mentioned), that it is rash to assume that Varro is simply representing the position of Antiochus on philosophical questions, is surely quite absurd. Varro was indeed a very learned man in many areas, but in philosophy he is attested, by both Cicero and Augustine, on the basis of evidence available to them, to be a thoroughgoing disciple of Antiochus, and there is no reason to doubt this. There is a useful discussion of this passage in Tarrant (1995), pp. 79–82.

[20] Augustine is quoting here from the final book of Varro's vast compilation *Antiquitates rerum humanarum et divinarum*, in 41 books, the last 15 of which concerned divine matters. In this final book, he discussed 'select gods', that is, the central deities of the Greco-Roman pantheon. I employ here the Penguin translation of Henry Bettenson.

[21] That, it would seem from *CD* 6.3, means the fourth book of the second part of the *Antiquitates*, and the twenty-ninth of the whole work.

[22] Here Augustine slips in a bit of propaganda for his own (Christian) position. In fact, we see here Varro adopting, as did Antiochus, the basic Stoic distinction between an active and passive principle in the universe, symbolizing the first by the sky and masculine divinities, the latter by the earth and feminine divinities. There is no question of postulating a further, higher divinity, 'who created both'.

[23] That is to say, Book 40, in which he discussed 'uncertain gods', that is, divinities which it is difficult to identify with certainty. The identity of the Kabeiroi, the Great Gods of Samothrace, was quite uncertain, since they were pre-Indo-European entities, but conjecture linked them with the Dioscuri, who had a heavenly and a chthonic aspect.

He starts by making a solemn undertaking (adopting a kind of religious tone of voice) that he will explain those teachings in writing and convey their meaning to the Samothracians themselves, who do not understand their purport. He says, in fact, that a study of the evidence in Samothrace leads to the conclusion that one of their images represented the sky, another the earth, another the archetypes which Plato called 'forms'. He urges that Jupiter should be understood as the sky, Juno as the earth, Minerva as the forms; the sky being maker, the earth material, the forms providing the patterns for creation. I pass over the fact that Plato ascribes such importance to his 'forms' that, according to him, the sky does not create anything, using them as patterns; in fact it is itself so created.

Augustine tries here to confute Varro by appealing to a literal interpretation of Plato's *Timaeus*, in accordance with which the heavens are created with the rest of the world (*Ti.* 37D), but this just serves to point up the fact that Varro/Antiochus is basing himself on a de-mythologized, Stoicized interpretation of the same dialogue, according to which the Demiurge becomes the Stoic active principle (*to poioun*), while the Receptacle becomes the passive principle, and the Paradigm the active principle's creative reason-principles, or *logoi*.

What we may note in particular about this piece of allegorization by Varro is the natural and uncontroversial way in which he introduces the conception that Minerva (Athena), springing as she does from the head of Zeus, may represent the totality of Forms as thoughts of God. Varro is not trying to introduce his readers to this concept as something innovative; rather, he is making use of it, as something he expects to be well recognized, as a basis for delivering an allegorization of the Great Gods of Samothrace. This should surely tell us something about the degree of acceptability of the concept of the Forms as thoughts of God in the intellectual circle which Varro is addressing.

So then, I would maintain, a Stoicized version of the doctrine of the Forms as thoughts of God is a feature of the Platonism propounded by Antiochus of Ascalon. Let us move on from this, then, to observe its next manifestation.

This occurs in the works of the Platonizing Alexandrian Jewish philosopher Philo, a half-century after Antiochus. Philo is actually the first author unequivocally to present the formulation of Forms as thoughts of God, and this circumstance has unfortunately seduced some Philo scholars, such as Roberto Radice of Milan, in his study *Platonismo e creazionismo in Filone di Alessandria*,[24] to claim him as the inventor of it. While this notion is plainly quite untenable, there is yet a certain amount for which Philo may perhaps be given credit. Philo inherits a Platonism which seems to have evolved somewhat from the solidly Stoicized metaphysics propounded by Antiochus towards a renewed concept of the transcendence and immateriality of God, helped on its way, it would seem, by the revival, in the mid-first century BCE, of the Pythagorean tradition, which may be associated with the figure of Eudorus of Alexandria, an older contemporary of Philo's, with whom he may even have been personally acquainted. At any rate, we find in Philo, particularly in such a work as the *De Opificio Mundi,* a system involving a transcendent supreme God, an intelligible world (*kosmos noêtos*), presented as the 'internal reason' (*logos endiathetos*) of God, and a Logos that goes forth and creates the physical cosmos (*logos prophorikos*), and thereafter holds it together. At *Opif.* 16,[25] for instance, we find the following description of God's creative activity:

> For God, because he is God, understood in advance that a beautiful copy (*mimêma*) would not come into existence apart from a beautiful model (*paradeigma*), and that none of the objects of sense-perception would be without fault, unless it was modeled on the archetypal and intelligible Idea. Having resolved to create this visible world of ours, He fashioned first the intelligible world, in order that in fashioning the physical world he might be able to use an immaterial and most godlike model, producing from this older model a younger copy which would contain within itself as many sensible classes of being as there were intelligible ones in the original.

This plainly owes much to the *Timaeus* (28A–B, 48E, etc.), but with the significant difference that now the paradigm is nothing other

---

[24] Radice (1989).
[25] Here I borrow the Loeb translation of F.H. Colson, *Philon* i., v. i, *On the Creation* (*De Opificio Mundi*) (Cambridge, MA, 2014).

than the contents of the divine intellect. Philo goes on (17–18) to present us with the vivid image of an architect being commissioned to build a fine city, with all its accoutrements (he probably has the original planning of Alexandria in mind!), and carrying round the whole plan of the city in his head as a model in accordance to which he can refer when laying out the physical city. Such is God's situation with regard to the physical universe. Now, the elaboration of this exemplum is no doubt Philo's own work, but the exemplum itself may not be original to him. It bears a certain similarity to the exemplum used by Cicero in *Orator* 8, which adduces Pheidias and his statues of Zeus and Athena, and which may well derive from Antiochus (though the 'austere' school of thought would demur on this, since Antiochus is not referred to); but there is also the significant difference that Pheidias is presumed to be contemplating something like a 'Platonic' Form of the divinity concerned, whereas the architect is simply drawing on his own expertise. However, as we shall see in a moment, both images seem to be combined in the reference to the artist adduced by Alcinous, in ch. 9 of his *Didaskalikos,* to which we may now turn.

There is much more evidence, of course, to be derived from Philo, but I take it that on this occasion I am not so much delivering a general survey of the concept of the Forms as thoughts of God in the later Platonist tradition as trying to establish its provenance, so we may spare ourselves a full investigation of Philo's employment of the concept. On the face of it, his main contribution (though I do not believe that it is original to himself)[26] is the concept of the intelligible world (*kosmos noêtos*) – although even this is not much more than a de-mythologization of the 'intelligible living being' (*noêton zôion*) of *Ti.* 30C–31B.

Let us turn instead to a consideration of Alcinous. Alcinous (now that we are no longer allowed to identify him with Albinus) is a slightly mysterious figure, but he may reasonably be situated in the mid-second century CE, and his *Didaskalikos,* or 'Handbook of

---

[26] We may note that Timaeus Locrus uses the phrase *idanikos kosmos* (§30), and TL is hardly likely to be dependent on Philo, even if he post-dates him. The influence is more likely to be the other way about (Philo does at least know of pseudo-Pythagoric writings, such as that of Ocellus Lucanus (cf. *On the Eternity of the World,* 12).

Platonism', does not aspire to be a work of any originality – indeed, there is some evidence (including one more or less verbatim passage in ch. 12) that his work is essentially an 'update' of a similar work by Arius Didymus, back in the late first century BCE.[27] At any rate, there can be little chance that he is in any way influenced by Philo.

What he presents us with, in ch. 9, is a fairly bald summary of Platonist doctrine on the Forms. It is worth quoting this at some length:[28]

> Matter constitutes one principle,[29] but Plato postulates others also, to wit, the paradigmatic, that is the Forms, and that constituted by God, the father and cause of all things. Form (*idea*) is considered, in relation to God, his thinking (*noêsis*); in relation to us, the primary object of thought (*prôton noêton*); in relation to matter, measure (*metron*); in relation to the sensible world, its paradigm; and in relation to itself, essence. For in general everything that we can conceptualize must come to be in reference to something of which the model (*paradeigma*) must pre-exist, just as if one thing were to be derived from another, in the way that my image derives from me; and even if the model does not always subsist eternally, in any event every artist, having the model within himself, applies the structure of it to matter.

He goes on to say, just below, in connection with the question 'Of what things are there Forms?,' that 'The Forms are the eternal and perfect thoughts of God.' And just below that again, in relation to the question 'Are there such things as Forms?,' he argues: 'Whether God is an intellect or possessed of an intellect, he has thoughts, and these are eternal and unchanging; and if this is the case, Forms exist.'

We see here the theory of Forms as thoughts of God in what one might term its 'classical' or fully fledged form, presented by Alcinous as basic Platonic doctrine. Indeed, the proposition that, since God is either an intellect or at least possessed of an intellect, he must necessarily have thoughts is used as the premiss for a further conclusion, that there are such things as Forms at all. We may note also the passing allusion to the exemplum of the artist having

---

[27] *Pace* Göransson (1995), who produces some good negative arguments, but does not ultimately convince me.
[28] The translation is my own, from (1993).
[29] He has dealt with this in the previous chapter.

a conception in his mind, which he then transfers to canvass, or embodies in stone or bronze. This seems to form a bridge between Cicero's Pheidias example and Philo's architect, and indicates that the image was by Alcinous' time a fairly well-worn one, in support of the argument for the Forms being divine thoughts.

In Plutarch also, somewhat earlier than Alcinous, the premiss that the Forms are divine thoughts or *logoi* turns up at a number of points in the corpus, though never (in the surviving works) quite as directly as we find in Alcinous. In the *De sera numinis vindicta*, for example (550D), we find a description of God setting himself up as a paradigm for all moral goodness, and thus establishing that the pursuit of virtue is nothing else than 'assimilation to God' (*homoiôsis theôi*). This is not as clear as one might wish as a statement of the theory, but we may combine this with a striking passage from the *De Iside et Osiride* (373A–B), where Osiris is presented allegorically as the Logos of God, filled with *logoi* which impress themselves on matter 'like figures stamped on wax' (a reference to *Tht.* 191Cff.). Further, we find a distinction made between the 'soul' and the 'body' of Osiris, the former being the Logos as residing within the mind of God, the latter the Logos in its emanatory mode, infusing the physical world with its contents – a scenario, indeed, very like that which we found in Philo a few generations earlier.

One finds a somewhat clearer exposition of the doctrine, in fact, in the works of the later Athenian Platonist Atticus, in the second half of the second century. In the course of a polemical treatise entitled *Against Those Who Claim to Interpret Plato through Aristotle,*[30] extensive passages of which have been preserved for us by the ecclesiastical writer Eusebius of Caesarea, he has occasion to commend Plato's Theory of Forms (Fr. 7 Baudry):

> It is just in this respect that Plato surpasses all others. Discerning, in relation to the Forms, that God is Father and Creator and lord and guardian of all things, and recognizing, on the analogy of material creations, that the craftsman (*dêmiourgos*) first forms a conception (*noêsai*) of that which he is proposing to create, and then, once he has

---

[30] Probably directed against his contemporary, the Peripatetic Aristocles, the teacher of Alexander of Aphrodisias, who had had the audacity to compose a work (also quoted by Eusebius) commending Plato as a promising but imperfect predecessor of Aristotle.

formed his conception, applies this likeness to the material, he concludes by analogy that the thoughts (*noêmata*) of God are anterior to material objects, models (*paradeigmata*) of the things that come to be, immaterial and intelligible, always remaining identically the same.

This seems to touch all the right bases, alluding both to the *Timaeus* (God as Father and Maker, *dêmiourgos, paradeigmata*) and to the *Phaedo* ('always remaining identically the same'), while adducing the process of artistic or craftsmanly creation.

This is not quite the end of the story, however. There is a troubling report, emanating from Proclus (*In Tim.* 1, 394, 6ff. Diehl), *via* Porphyry, who should have known, criticizing Atticus for situating the Paradigm, as repository of the Forms, as distinct from, though inferior to, the Demiurge, whom he takes to be the supreme God. One does not know quite what to make of that, but it may be that Atticus, in wishing to preserve the objective reality of the Forms, saw no problem in postulating them as distinct from, though ontologically inferior to, his supreme deity, while also being intelligized by him.[31] At any rate, the problem of their exact status continued into the next century with Longinus, who was head of the Academy in Athens, and Porphyry's teacher before he came to Plotinus in Rome, and in ch. 18 of his *Life of Plotinus*, Porphyry tells against himself the story of his producing this doctrine in Plotinus' seminar, and, after a long debate, being converted to the Plotinian view that the Forms are in fact in the mind of the Demiurge – the only modification being, of course, that now the Demiurge is no longer the supreme principle, but a secondary one, Intellect, the One being superior to the Forms!

It would seem, then, that by the middle of second century CE there was very much of a consensus as to the nature of the Forms as thoughts in the mind of God, but that in the latter part of the

---

[31] Atticus is also criticized, we may note (along with Plutarch and Democritus the Platonist), by Syrianus, in his *Commentary on the Metaphysics* (p. 105, 35ff.), for holding 'that the Forms are universal reason-principles (*logoi*) subsisting eternally in the substance of the Soul; for even if they distinguish them from the commonalities (*koinotêtes*) present in sensible objects, nevertheless one should not confuse together the reason-principles in the soul and the so-called enmattered intellect (*enulos nous*) with the paradigmatic and immaterial Forms and demiurgic intellections'. This complicates the situation even further! See on all this the most judicious analysis of Alexandra Michalewski, in her fine monograph (2014).

century, with Atticus (and I suspect also with the Neopythagorean Numenius, whom I have left out of the present investigation),[32] the problem was beginning to arise: is this Creator God in whose mind the Forms reside really the highest God, or does perhaps the very fact of his intellection, comporting as it does something of a duality, preclude him from the radical unity that should be characteristic of a supreme divinity?

There seems a nice irony in ending with a problem, even as we began with one, so I will draw this enquiry to a close at this point. We may note however, that, for Plotinus in the next century, it is unequivocally a secondary divine principle, Intellect, not the supreme principle, the One, that is the proper repository of Forms, as the self-thinking involved in cognizing these is regarded by Plotinus as incompatible with the radically unitary status of the first principle.

[32] Numenius' views would be interesting to discern, as he made a distinction (Frs. 12, 15 Des Places) between a supreme divinity, the 'Father', whom he describes as an Intellect *at rest* (*hestôs*), and a secondary one, the Demiurge, who is active in the work of creation. In which of them do the Forms reside? Possibly in both, in different modes, but we lack evidence on this point.

CHAPTER 4

The Hierarchy of Being as a Framework for Platonist Ethical Theory

From a consideration of metaphysical themes, we may turn now to the subject of Platonist ethical theory, though still with an eye to the metaphysical presuppositions on which such an ethical system is inevitably based. It is a notable feature of modern ethical theory that, with the demise of any religious or indeed systematically philosophical underpinning, efforts to establish a set of principles on which to proceed meet with considerable difficulty.[1] This is not a problem for ancient ethical systems, including the Platonist.

It has of course always been the case, from the time of Plato himself – if not that of Socrates – that Platonist ethical theory has been tied to a conception of the structure of reality, to wit, that there is a realm of true Being, presided over by a cosmic Intellect or rational World-Soul, the contents of which is a matrix of Forms, of which the physical realm of Becoming is a (necessarily imperfect) copy, or projection. The aim of human striving, the *telos* (in later terminology), consists in freeing ourselves as much as possible from physical concerns and passionate attachments while in the body, and a constant effort to develop that part of ourselves (sc. the rational soul) which most resembles the realm of true Being and its presiding Intellect, which may be termed God. To that extent, the aim of human striving may be described as being 'assimilation to God' (*homoiôsis theôi*), and this is properly achieved by the practice of the virtues, or of Virtue as a whole.[2]

---

[1] For a good, representative account of the state of play in the field of 'virtue ethics', which most nearly approximates to ancient ethical theories, see Swanton (2003).

[2] We must not, of course, neglect to recognize that Aristotle too, particularly in *Nicomachean Ethics*, 10.7, postulates that the practice of *theoria* assimilates us to divinity and brings about our true felicity (*eudaimonia*).

I trust that this rather bald account of Platonic ethical theory does not introduce any serious distortion into the situation as we may assume it to have obtained for the duration of the Old Academy – that is, down to about 275 BCE (though, under the third Scholarch, Polemon, there may already have occurred a shift in emphasis, as we shall see in a moment). Thereafter, two complications arose, which between them cover the next two centuries or so. The first is the turn to scepticism initiated by Arcesilaus, and carried on, with various modifications, down to the time of Philo of Larisa in the early part of the first century BCE, during which, if the Academy had a position on the *telos*, we have no clear view as to what it might have been.[3] The second results from the return to dogmatism initiated by Antiochus of Ascalon in the 80s BCE, where Antiochus, to all appearances, adopts as a *telos* the Stoic formulation of 'life in accordance with Nature' (cf. Cic. *De Fin.* 2.34), a doctrine which he has no hesitation in attributing at least to Polemon, last head of the Old Academy, as well as to Aristotle:

> And this is the fountain-head from which one's whole theory of goods and evils must necessarily flow. Polemon, and also before him Aristotle, held that the primary objects were the ones that I have just mentioned (sc. good health, sound mind, comfortable surroundings). Thus arose the doctrine of the Old Academy and of the Peripatetics, maintaining that the end of goods (*telos agathôn*) is to live in accordance with nature, that is, to enjoy the primary gifts of nature's bestowal with the accompaniment of virtue.[4]

This *telos,* as has often been noted, differs in no way from the Stoic one, except in respect of its relative upgrading of the goods of the body and external goods, and so does not, on the face of it, direct the individual to any realm of reality beyond the physical – though Antiochus may conceivably have thought that it did; it depends on how close to Stoicism he really was. Certainly, if he was at all justified in projecting such a formulation as 'life according to Nature' back

---

[3] The New Academics Arcesilaus and Carneades would seem to have propounded a *telos* of *eudaimonia,* 'happiness' or, more accurately, 'flourishing' (Sextus Empiricus, *AM* 7.158; 166), only with the proviso that this was based on no more than probability (*to pithanon*). It is attainable by *epokhê,* 'withholding of assent to impressions', which may or not be taken as compatible with 'assimilation to God', or indeed with 'living in concordance with Nature'.

[4] I borrow the Loeb translation of Rackham.

onto Polemon – as I am on record as suggesting that he may have been[5] – then this formulation of the *telos* need not exclude reference to a higher level of reality, if *physis* may be taken to refer to the nature of things in general, which for any Platonist worthy of the name must include a 'higher' realm of True Being.

Indeed, if we take into account an interesting passage from Cicero's *De Legibus* (1.25),[6] we can see an explicit connection being made, in a context exhibiting strong Antiochian traits,[7] between man and God through the practice of virtue. Cicero has just been asserting (1.23) that reason (*ratio, logos*) is something that humans share with God, so that following the law of Nature, which is an expression of divine Reason, also implies following God:

> Iam vero virtus eadem in homine ac deo est, neque alio ullo in genere praeterea; est autem virtus nihil aliud nisi perfecta et ad summum perducta natura: est igitur homini cum deo similitudo.

> Further, virtue is the same in man as in God, and in no other species apart from that.[8] Yet virtue is nothing else than one's nature made perfect and brought to a peak (of excellence): it constitutes therefore a likeness of man with God.

As Tarrant remarks (*loc. cit.*), this last sentence can just as well be – and normally has been – rendered, '[T]here is therefore a likeness of man with God,' but in fact, as he maintains, in the context, either rendering conveys the same message, that the practice of the virtues, like the obedience to natural law mentioned previously, does not just bring us into concordance with Nature, but constitutes an assimilation of man to God. There would not therefore necessarily be so radical a distinction between the Antiochian *telos* of 'concordance with Nature' and the later Platonist formula of 'assimilation to God'.[9]

---

[5] See Dillon (2003), pp. 160–5.
[6] Recently discussed by Harold Tarrant, in a most useful article (2007), pp. 421–4. We also find this conjunction manifesting itself interestingly in Philo of Alexandria, e.g. *Migr.* 128 – attributed, characteristically, to Moses.
[7] Cf. my remarks at (1977), p. 80.
[8] This presumably is not to deny that other animals may exhibit 'natural' virtues of one sort or another; simply that such virtues, lacking rationality as they do, have nothing in common with God.
[9] I would therefore be inclined to modify my position as presented in *The Middle Platonists* (e.g. pp. 122–3), in the light of this passage from the *De Legibus,* for the appreciation of the

However this may be, with the next generation of Platonists, represented by Eudorus of Alexandria,[10] the formulation of the *telos* is revised in a more overtly other-worldly, or 'vertical' direction, as opposed to the more apparently 'horizontal', Stoicizing one of Antiochus. In fact, Eudorus seems to be the first, in later times,[11] to revive the formula derived from Plato's *Theaetetus* 176B: 'assimilation to God *in so far as that is possible* (*homoiôsis theôi kata to dynaton*)', though with what seems to be an interesting modification, as we shall see. The text in Stobaeus is as follows (2, 49, 8ff.):

> Socrates and Plato agree with Pythagoras that the *telos* is 'assimilation to God'. Plato, however, defined this more clearly by adding 'according as is possible', and it is only possible by means of wisdom, that is to say, in accordance with virtue. For it is the role of God to create the cosmos and to administer the cosmos, while the role of the wise man is the establishment of a life-style and the conduct of a life – something that seems to be hinted at by Homer when he says, 'he followed in the footsteps of the goddess' (*Od.* 5.193; 7.38).[12]

There are various notable aspects of this passage. First is the explicit linking of Plato (and Socrates!), not with Aristotle and the Stoics, as would have been the tendency of Antiochus, but with Pythagoras. Such a connection would not, of course, have been alien to the tendencies of either Speusippus or Xenocrates, but does represent a deviation from that of Antiochus.

significance of which I am indebted to Harold Tarrant. One might add that the fact that Philo of Alexandria – an eclectic thinker, to be sure, but not mindlessly so – is prepared to adopt both formulations of the *telos* at various points ('likeness to God', e.g at *Fug.* 63 and 'concordance with nature', e.g. at *Dec.* 81, as well as both together at *Migr.* 128) is a further indication that the latter can be interpreted in terms of the former.

[10] That is to say, if we can accept, as I would still maintain (cf. (1977), p. 116), that the series of *problêmata* set out by Arius Didymus (*ap.* Stob. *Anthol.* 2, 45, 7ff., following on his account of the ethical section of Eudorus' *Diairesis tou kata philosophian logou*, which he tells us was presented *problêmatikôs*, still represent Eudoran doctrine. This assumption has been challenged by Göransson (1995), though without adequate justification, it seems to me – like much else in that curious book.

[11] We cannot, I think, be sure that this formulation was ever adopted in any formal way as a definition of the purpose of life in the period of the Old Academy, simply because the idea of defining a *telos agathôn*, or 'end of goods', as such does not seem to predate the Stoics, but on the other hand, as we have seen, Antiochus is determined to credit Polemon with a prefiguration of the Stoic *telos*, so we must recognize the possibility.

[12] Philo also makes an allusion to this Homeric passage at *Migr.* 128: 'whenever the mind, having entered on virtue's path, walks in the track (*kat' ikhnos*) of right reason and follows God'.

Then, there is the expression *kata to dynaton*, which, in the mouth of Socrates in the *Theaetetus*, pretty plainly constituted a modest disclaimer of the possibility of complete *homoiôsis* with God, but which for Eudorus becomes rather a specification of precisely that faculty within us in virtue of which we *can* become like God, to wit, the intellect – taking *phronêsis* to represent intellectual activity. This, it must be said, is not an entirely unreasonable interpretation of the Greek, in view of the immediately following sentence in Plato's text: 'and assimilation implies becoming just and holy with the help of wisdom (*phronêsis*)'; but nonetheless it would seem that modern interpreters are almost certainly correct in taking *kata to dynaton* as a modest disclaimer, and that what we are seeing here is an example of a scholastic tendency, dominant much later, in the Neoplatonic period, but also, plainly, manifesting itself already in the first century BCE, in accordance with which every utterance of the divine Plato is given its full semantic weight, regardless of the idiomatic probabilities.

The manner of our *homoiôsis* with God is now developed in an interesting way, the wise man's[13] establishment of a life-style (*katastasis biou*) being assimilated to God's creation of the cosmos, and his maintenance of his life (*zôês diagôgê*)[14] to God's administration of the cosmos – Arius (or Eudorus?) in the process employing two jaw-breaking compounds, the latter of which, *kosmodioikêtikos*, is attested nowhere else.[15] Presumably the 'establishment of a life-style' denotes the adoption of a life according to virtue, which involves bringing one's life to order out of disorder, that being analogous to God's organizing of a cosmos out of chaos (whether pre-existent or not).[16]

Arius/Eudorus now goes on (*ap.* Stob. 2, 49, 16ff.) to distinguish three modes in which Plato presents the *telos,* corresponding to the

---

[13] We may note that here only the *sophos* is to be compared to God, not every man; but that is fair enough, since the comparison is based on the practice of virtue.

[14] The distinction between *bios* and *zôê* is presumably to be interpreted in this way.

[15] We may leave aside, in the present context, whether this comparison does or does not imply a commitment to a doctrine of temporal creation. I think that it does not; but it does indicate that the Demiurge of the *Timaeus* is to be identified as the supreme deity.

[16] The final element in the passage, the adducing of a proof-text from Homer, in the form of the description of Odysseus' following in the footsteps of Kalypso in Book 5 of the *Odyssey,* and, perhaps more significantly, Athena (disguised as a little girl), in Book 7, need not concern us at present, though it is a useful early indication of the allegorization of Homer in a Platonist, rather than a Stoic, mode.

three divisions of philosophy first laid down (at least explicitly) by Xenocrates, physics, ethics and logic. The 'physical' mode is discerned at the end of the *Timaeus* (90A–D), where indeed, in 90D in particular, all the key terms are employed: *xynhepomenon, exhomoiôsai, telos* – this last being the only place in which *telos* is used by Plato in this connection.[17] It is deemed 'physical', presumably, as being presented in the context of an exposition of the structure of the universe – the *Timaeus,* of course, being accorded the subtitle *physikos* in the edition of Thrasyllus.

For Eudorus, the properly 'ethical' version of the *telos* is presented in *Rep.* 10, 613A,[18] where Socrates states, in the context of asserting the happiness of the just man: 'For the gods never neglect anyone who is prepared to devote himself to becoming just and, by practising virtue, to assimilate himself to God (*homoiousthai theôi*) as much as is humanly possible (*eis hoson dynaton anthrôpôi*).' Once again, this is in accord with the classification followed by Thrasyllus, the *Republic* being classed as *politikos,* 'politics' being a subdivision of ethics.

Lastly, the *Theaetetus* passage is presented as the *telos* from a 'logical' perspective, presumably because here the argument for fleeing this realm of existence and assimilating oneself to God is based on the premiss that in this realm 'there must always be some element opposed to the good' – and perhaps because the dialogue was viewed in Eudorus' day as being concerned primarily with logic and epistemology (its characterization in Thrasyllus' edition is *peirastikos*).

This slightly odd division of modes, as it may seem to us, is stimulated, no doubt, by a scholastic concern for completeness. The divine Plato must be seen to have propounded the *telos* in all of the three recognized areas of philosophical enquiry – not, we may note, in the order favoured by Antiochus (cf. Cic. *Acad. Pr.* 19), which was Ethics, Physics, and Logic, but in that originally propounded by Xenocrates (cf. Sextus, *Against the Logicians* 1.16): Physics, Ethics, Logic.

---

[17] We may note also the phrase, in 90C, 'in so far as human nature is capable of sharing in immortality', which provides evidence, if such were needed, of the essentially cautionary sense of *kata to dynaton* at *Tht.* 176B.

[18] Wachsmuth plumps rather for the passages 9, 585B–C, and 10, 608Cff., but with less plausibility – though they are not irrelevant to the overall theme. Another interesting passage, it must be said, is 6, 490A–B, where we find mention of the appropriate part of the human soul striving towards, not God precisely, but Truth, viz, the realm of Forms.

Such, then, is the situation as regards the relation of ethical theory to the structure of reality at the beginning of the Middle Platonic period. We may turn now to the distinguished Platonist Plutarch of Chaeronea, active in the decades immediately before and after the turn of the first century CE. For Plutarch, the *telos* is unequivocally *homoiôsis theôi,* as we can observe from a notable passage of his *De Sera Numinis Vindicta* (550DE),[19] put into the mouth of his brother Timon, in which certain distinctive features are introduced into the doctrine:

> Consider first that God, as Plato says, offers himself to all as a pattern of every excellence, thus rendering human virtue, which is in some way or other an assimilation (*exhomoiôsis*) to himself, accessible to all who can 'follow God'. Indeed, this was the origin of the change whereby universal nature, disordered before, became a 'cosmos', through assimilation and participation, after a fashion, in the form and excellence associated with the divinity. The same philosopher says further that nature kindled vision in us so that the soul, behold-ing the motions of the heavenly bodies and wondering at the sight, should grow to accept and cherish all that moves in stateliness and order, and thus come to hate discordant and errant passions, and to shun the aimless and haphazard as source of all vice and jarring error; for man is fitted to derive from God no greater blessing than to become settled in virtue through copying and aspiring to the beauty and the goodness that are his.

As I say, there are a number of features of this manifesto worth noting. First of all, Plutarch gives a more personal slant to the process of assimilation to God by stating that 'God offers himself as a pattern', whereas in the central *Theaetetus* passage the emphasis is rather on the necessity of our own efforts at *homoiôsis,* no mention being made of divine activity. Even at 176E, where there is mention of a *paradeigma* – or rather two *paradeigmata,* a divine one and a godless one – the *paradeigma* is just standing there; there is no emphasis on its being *put* there. We can observe here, therefore, I think, a greater stress being placed by Plutarch on God's agency than is present in the text of Plato.

Then, we can see Plutarch introducing into the scenario his own doctrine of pre-cosmic chaos, with the implication that not only the

---

[19] I borrow the Loeb translation of F.C. Babbitt, *Moralia,* book 7, ch. 41.

individual human soul, but also the World-Soul (*alias* universal nature), is being drawn by God into likeness with himself.[20] This is a further extension of the original concept of *homoiôsis theôi* as presented by Plato, though one that he doubtless would have approved, providing as it does a cosmic backdrop to the application of it to the individual.

Lastly, there is the linking of the *homoiôsis*-doctrine with the description in the *Timaeus* (45B; 47A–C) of the bestowal upon mortals of the faculty of sight by the Young Gods (though here Plutarch attributes this to Nature), which has the purpose of bringing to order the disorderly impulses of our souls. Here again, there is nothing with which Plato would have any quarrel, but the whole passage provides evidence of the degree of systematization of Platonic doctrine that had taken place over the intervening centuries.[21]

We can gather from the evidence of Plutarch, then, that the linking of ethical doctrine with a theory of a hierarchy of being has been significantly strengthened and systematized by the latter part of the first century CE. Let us turn next to Alcinous' *Didaskalikos,* or *Handbook of Platonism,* to see how things stand in the mid-second century. With Alcinous, I think we can see that there comes to the fore a certain tension inherent in the ideal of *homoiôsis theôi* which had been obscured hitherto, even in Plutarch, and which is nicely expressed by Julia Annas, in her most useful, and to some extent ground-breaking, study, *Platonic Ethics, Old and New* (1999). She is worth quoting at some length (pp. 63–4):

> The idea of virtue as becoming like God can be interpreted in different ways, and Plato shows no awareness of the differences. Nor do the Middle Platonists; Alcinous, for example, puts various

---

[20] We find also a nice passage in the *Life of Dion,* ch. 10. 2 (drawn attention to by De Lacy and Einarson *ad loc.*), where Plutarch portrays Dion as trying to induce Dionysius II to submit himself to the instruction of Plato, 'in order that his character might be regulated by the principles of virtue, and that he might be conformed to that divinest and most beautiful model of all being, in obedience to whose direction the universe issues from disorder into order' – once again giving a cosmic dimension to *homoiôsis theôi.*

[21] There is also interesting evidence, once again adduced by De Lacy and Einarson, of Plutarch's use here, not only of the *Timaeus* itself but of the pseudo-Pythagorean treatise of Timaeus Locrus, *On the Nature of the World,* ch. 11, since Plutarch's use of 'kindle' (*anapsai*) and of the phrase 'beholding the motions of the heavenly bodies' echoes similar phraseology in Timaeus Locrus, and not anything in the *Timaeus.*

passages together as though they obviously supported a single idea. Before being condescending, however, we should reflect that the difference between these positions is apparent to us because we find the idea of becoming like God strange, and therefore probe the contexts where we find it in order to discover how to interpret it. To Plato and ancient Platonists, on the other hand, the idea that becoming virtuous is becoming like God, and the associated idea that becoming like God or the divine is living in a way that identifies oneself with one's reasoning, were clearly both intuitively obvious and emotionally compelling – two features that might explain why we do not find more sensitivity to the different forms the idea takes.

Part of the reason for this may be an indeterminacy here in the idea of God. If becoming like God is living in accordance with your reason, then it need imply no more than a very ordinary, indeed traditional practice of virtue, understood as rational activity. God here is just reason, understood as the divine in us, with no implication that reason is actually different from what we already supposed it to be, namely something which can guide practice as well as theory. But if becoming like God is actually a flight from the mix of good and evil in our world, then God is being thought of rather differently, as something perfectly good outside human experience and not to be characterized in human terms, but which nonetheless it makes sense for humans to try to emulate.

Now Annas here, it seems to me, is putting her finger on a most important point of tension within the concept of *homoiôsis theôi*. The tension does not, indeed, seem to be recognized in the thinkers whom we have been examining up to this, but Annas is, I think, not being quite fair to Alcinous.[22] Alcinous does certainly seem to reflect, at least, some degree of speculation along these lines by contemporary Platonist thinkers. How, people must have asked, does the practice of the four cardinal virtues bring us closer to a God who cannot be supposed to exercise, or have any need of, these virtues, at least in the form familiar to us? Plotinus, a century later, in *Ennead* I 2, deals with this problem by postulating a system of levels of virtue,[23] and granting the gods *paradigmatic* equivalents of 'purificatory' (*kathartikai*)

---

[22] She actually recognizes this, albeit somewhat grudgingly, just below, when she says: 'A Platonist like Alcinous is vaguely aware of a difficulty here, which emerges in a worry as to which God a virtuous person is likened to' (p. 64).

[23] I have discussed this topic in Dillon (1983).

levels of the four virtues, but there is really no sign of such a solution among Platonists of the Middle Platonic period. Alcinous' solution is as follows (ch. 28, 181, 36–45):

> Sometimes he (sc. Plato) says that the end is to liken oneself to God, but sometimes that it consists in following him, as when he says (*Laws* 4, 715E): 'God who, as old tradition has it, holds the beginning and the end', etc.; and sometimes both, as when he says (*Phdr.* 248A): 'The soul that follows and likens itself to God', and so on. For certainly the beginning of advantage is the good, and this is dependent on God; so, following on from this beginning, the end (*telos*) would be likening oneself to God – *by which we mean, obviously, the god in the heavens, not, of course, the god above the heavens, who does not possess virtue, being superior to this.*

This solution to the problem, of course, is only available if one is able to postulate a distinction between a god 'in the heavens' and a god 'above the heavens', and that does not seem to have been open to Eudorus, for whom the supreme deity seems still be a Timaean Demiurge-figure.[24] Indeed, before the second century, there is little sign of a hierarchy of divinities or principles in the Platonist system.[25] Plutarch, admittedly, toys at various places in his works with a secondary divinity,[26] but it is a rather more ambiguous figure than what I am in search of here, and he does not bring it into connection with his treatment of the *telos*. Only really with Numenius, probably a contemporary of Alcinous in the later second century, do we find a clear distinction between a primary and a secondary God, only the latter of whom is directly concerned with the administration of the world (e.g. Frs. 12, 15 Des Places), but on the other hand we do not know that he related this to his specification of the *telos*, simply because, sadly, we have no information as to Numenius' ethical doctrines – though it is more or less certain that he would have adopted the *telos* of *homoiôsis theôi*.

---

[24] This despite a distinction which he is reported as making (*ap.* Simpl. *In Phys.* 181, 10ff. Diels) between a supreme One and a Monad partnering a Dyad.

[25] I do not wish here to count a Logos or a World-Soul as a secondary divinity, though they do serve, importantly, as intermediaries, as for instance in the system of Philo of Alexandria.

[26] I am thinking primarily of the curious appearance of the figure of Dionysus, as opposed to Apollo, in the *De E apud Delphos* (394A), who takes on something of the characteristics of a sublunary demiurge.

The tension therefore remains largely unresolved in the Middle Platonic period, although Alcinous has certainly identified the problem of being assimilated to the 'god above the heavens' (*hyperouranios theos*). What is concealed here, but comes out clearly in Plotinus' treatment of the subject, is the primarily self-centred nature of Platonist ethics, which is concerned specifically with the subordination of the passions to the reason, and the extrication of the individual from all ties to the material world. To criticize this from a Judaeo-Christian perspective, however, is hardly relevant, it seems to me, to our present purposes.

CHAPTER 5

Carneades the Socratic

Introduction

I wish to explore in this chapter[1] a topic which, though it has received considerable attention over the years,[2] has not, I think, been approached from quite the present angle, to wit, the degree to which that movement within Platonism known as the 'New Academy', or the sceptical Academy, can be seen, and indeed saw themselves, as constituting a return to the Socratic roots of Platonism, which had been progressively obscured by the increasing dogmatism of what we know as the 'Old' Academy, of Speusippus, Xenocrates, Polemon and their colleagues. In particular, I wish to explore the possibility that Carneades of Cyrene (*c.* 214–129 BCE), with whom the 'New Academic' tendency may be said to come to its culmination,[3] may have been encouraged to develop his theory of progressive degrees of 'probability' (insofar as that is a permissible translation of *pithanotês*)[4] on the basis of his study and interpretation of certain positions taken up by the Platonic Socrates in a number of the 'early' and 'middle' dialogues.

---

[1] This chapter began life as the 2014 Gregory Vlastos Memorial Lecture, at Queen's University, Kingston ON, which explains the relative, though I trust not undue, prominence given to Gregory Vlastos in the course of it.

[2] To mention only a selection of authorities: Long (1967), Stough (1969), Frede (1983), Ioppolo (1986), Bett (1989).

[3] The Academy of Arcesilaus and his immediate successors, we may note, is often described in the sources (e.g. Sextus Empiricus, *PH* 1.220) as 'Middle', rather than 'New', a title that is reserved for that of Carneades and *his* immediate successors.

[4] 'Persuasiveness' is perhaps a more accurate rendering, and I shall employ it henceforth; at any rate, any suggestion of *statistical* probability must be set aside in this context, as Myles Burnyeat has brought to our attention is his unpublished paper, 'Carneades was no Probabilist'.

It was, as we know, a basic principle propounded by Gregory Vlastos that one can identify in certain 'early' Platonic dialogues a philosophical method and a collection of philosophical theses which may properly be attributed to Socrates, as distinct from Plato. He explores these in a series of well-known articles and books,[5] often correcting himself sternly on matters of detail, but holding throughout to certain main theses. One of those, which is of particular relevance to the present enquiry, is that, despite Socrates' repeated and notorious disavowals of knowledge, there is in fact much that he feels he 'knows', at least in a certain sense of 'know'. What I wish to do first, on this occasion, is to review a series of key passages, chiefly from the *Apology* and the *Gorgias*, all of them well known to any Socratic scholar and dwelt on repeatedly by Vlastos, which both set up the apparent paradox of Socrates' avowal of ignorance combined with various assertions of deep conviction, as well as pointing to its solution – my thesis being that, if Gregory Vlastos could discern the solution to the paradox, then so could an ancient Platonist such as Carneades.

Socrates

Vasilis Politis, in a penetrating study of Plato's portrayal of the Socratic aporetic method in the early dialogues, *The Structure of Inquiry in Plato's Early Dialogues*,[6] identifies two extreme positions in Socratic studies, 'Socrates the Sceptic' and 'Socrates the Visionary', which he identifies respectively with Michael Forster[7] and Catherine Rowett (formerly Osborne)[8], but which of course go back much further than either of those protagonists. The former argues that the purpose of Socrates' aporetic enquiries is to prove that knowledge, primarily in the sphere of ethics, but also in all matters of consequence, is unattainable for mortals, and possible only for God, or the gods; the latter wishes to claim that, on the contrary, the point of Socrates' procedure is to indicate that we do not need to possess 'conventional', *propositional* knowledge in order to be wise, or happy,

---

[5] Chiefly, (1991) and (1994) – the latter containing revised versions of a number of important earlier papers. It is to this latter work that I will be mainly turning.

[6] (2015), p. 10.   [7] In Forster (2006), pp. 1–47, and (2007), pp. 1–35.

[8] In Rowett (2014).

but rather that the aim of Socratic dialectic is to enable us to attain a different kind of knowledge, namely, a direct, non-discursive *vision* of the truth, such as is vouchsafed, for example, to the Guardians of the *Republic* after their full course of dialectic.

For either of these positions numerous passages from the early dialogues can be adduced, but Politis would prefer to set them both aside for a position somewhere in the middle, and I must say that I would agree with him. The great question, though, is: just how is that position to be formulated?

We are all familiar, no doubt, with the famous passage in the *Apology* (21B–23B), where Socrates relates to the jury how he came to take on what he regards as his mission, which is to go about the city of Athens, questioning all those in society who have a pretension to knowledge, or expertise, in some field or other, and to demonstrate to them, by the well-directed employment of the method of *elenchus* which he has developed, that they cannot give a coherent account of what they think they know – with the purpose, it must be stressed, of bringing them to a healthier frame of mind, and making them better persons. His official conclusion, let us remind ourselves, is fairly uncompromising (23A–B):

> But the truth of the matter, gentlemen, is pretty certainly this, that in truth only God[9] is wise, and this oracle of his is his way of telling us that human wisdom (*anthrôpinê sophia*) has little or no value. It seems to me that he is not referring literally to Socrates, but has merely taken my name as an example, as if he would say to us, 'The wisest of you men is he who has realized, like Socrates, that in respect of wisdom he is really worthless.'[10]

But that is not in fact the whole story, even in the *Apology*. Later in the speech (29C–30B), when Socrates is specifying to the jury that, with all respect to them, he is not prepared, even if he were offered a free pardon on this occasion, on condition that he give up his annoying life-style, to accept any such conditions, he makes what

[9] I am conscious here that rendering *ho theos* as 'God' could be regarded as rather excessively monotheistic, and that it could be translated simply as 'the god', as referring to Apollo, but I think that Plato (whatever about Socrates) is really intending something more general by this expression, sc. 'the divinity'.

[10] I borrow the translation of H. Tredennick, *The Last Days of Socrates. The Apology, Crito, Phaedo* (London, 1954), slightly emended.

seems to me a most revealing admission: he is not actually concerned primarily to prove to himself and to others that no human has access to anything worthy of the title of knowledge; he is concerned rather to direct his fellow Athenians to the care of what is truly valuable in them, their souls (29D):[11]

> Well, supposing, as I said, that you should offer to acquit me on these terms, I should reply, 'Gentlemen, I am your very grateful and devoted servant, but I owe a greater obedience to God than to you, and so long as I draw breath and have my faculties, I shall never stop philosophizing and exhorting you and demonstrating (*endeiknumenos*) to everyone that I meet. I shall go on saying, in my usual way, "My very good friend, you are an Athenian and belong to a city which is the greatest and most famous in the world for its wisdom and strength. Are you not ashamed that you give your attention to acquiring as much money as possible, and similarly with reputation and honour, and give no attention or thought to understanding (*phronêsis*) and truth (*alêtheia*) and to your soul, that it may be as good as possible?"'

It seems to me here that Plato has allowed Socrates' position to change significantly, and that in the process he rather gives the game away as regards Socrates' profession to be solely concerned with pursuing the meaning of the riddling utterance of Apollo; his mission is really a much more positive one, with the *elenchus* simply serving as its preliminary, 'softening-up' strategy.[12] His true mission is to bring his fellow-citizens to a better frame of mind, where they honour the goods of the soul above either those of the body or external goods, and care for their souls as the one truly valuable part of their persons.

---

[11] *Ibid.,* slightly emended.

[12] It has always seemed to me, I must say, that there is something fishy about Socrates' claim that it was Chaerephon's question to the god that started him on his sacred mission, and I doubt that the jury fell for it for a moment (nor would it have improved their mood!). For one thing, why on earth would Chaerephon have asked his question, and indeed have been such a fan of Socrates in the first place, had not Socrates for some considerable time already been the Socrates that we all know and love, behaving in a thoroughly Socratic manner? I do not doubt that the incident with the Oracle took place, but the very fact that it did surely undermines Socrates' account of his motivation. In fact, it seems to me that we have here a good example of Vlastos' category of 'complex irony' (cf. *Socrates* (1991), Chapter 1, pp. 31ff.): beneath this teasing story there lies a serious belief of Socrates', that he has been in some sense called by God to disabuse pompous technical 'experts' – and indeed men in general – of their false conceit of knowledge.

This mission, moreover, involves a good deal of positive doctrine, or at least 'working hypotheses'. Indeed, Socrates, in the passage quoted above, speaks of himself as, not just 'philosophizing' (*philosophôn*) and 'exhorting' (*parakeleuomenos*), but also of 'demonstrating' (*endeiknumenos*) – which latter is a particularly strong didactic term to use. An *endeixis*, after all, is, in legal contexts, something like a 'writ of indictment', indicating the offence complained of, whereas in more general contexts it seems to mean something like 'proof' or 'demonstration'. The god Dionysus, you may recall, in the prologue of Euripides' *Bacchae* (lines 47–8), declares his (very grim) intentions in these terms:

> Wherefore I shall demonstrate (*endeixomai*) to him (sc. Pentheus),
> and to all the Thebans, that I was born a god.

– and this he proceeds to do, with devastating effect. Otherwise, the verb is most commonly used by the orators (Demosthenes, Aeschines, Andocides etc.) in legal contexts.

So this is an interesting verb for Plato to put into Socrates' mouth here. And it is clear from what Socrates says just below (29E) that he means business:

> And if any of you disputes this (sc. that one is not caring about one's soul) and professes to care about these things, I shall not at once let him go or leave him. No, I shall question him and examine him (*exetasô*) and test him (*elenxô*); and if it appears that, in spite of his profession, he has not attained to virtue (*kektêsthai aretên*), I shall reprove him for neglecting what is of supreme importance, and giving his chief attention to trivialities. I shall do this to everyone I meet, young or old, foreigner or fellow-citizen, but especially to you, my fellow-citizens, inasmuch as you are closer to me in kinship. For this, I do assure you, is what God commands, and it is my belief that no greater good has ever befallen you in this city than my service to God.[13]

There is, thus, plainly a set of principles in accordance with which Socrates is proceeding. On the basis of this passage, one might formulate the main ones as follows:

---

[13] I borrow the translation of H. Tredennick, *The Last Days of Socrates. The Apology, Crito, Phaedo* (London, 1954), slightly emended.

1. *Man is composed of soul and body, but the true identity and value of the individual resides in his or her soul.*[14]
2. *One should cultivate the 'goods' of the soul (viz., the virtues), while striving to free oneself from excessive attachment to 'lower' goods such as wealth and good reputation.*

On the basis of discussions in other dialogues, such as the *Protagoras* (352A–361D) and the *Meno* (86C–89C),[15] one might feel justified in adding:

3. *Virtue, or the virtues, have an intellectual basis, that is, they are forms of knowledge* (epistêmê), *or products of knowledge; and vice is therefore a product of ignorance.*[16]

– that is to say, that there is a rational basis for virtuous conduct, such that (a) it can be taught (which is what Socrates, presumably, feels that he is doing – although, when challenged, he would deny that he knows what virtue is, and is merely seeking a definition of it) and (b) all vicious behaviour is actually the product of ignorance, leading to the conclusion that 'no one does wrong willingly'.

We may add, I think, a further principle, this time from the *Gorgias* (472E ff.), to other aspects of which dialogue I will turn in a moment, to the effect that:

4. *It is better to suffer injustice than to inflict it – and, if one inflicts injustice, it is better to undergo punishment for that than to escape it.*

This is propounded in the dialogue primarily to annoy the sophist Polus, which it certainly succeeds in doing, but there can be little doubt that Plato intends this to be a conviction held by Socrates.

Indeed, it is in connection with this principle that Socrates, later in the dialogue, makes certain assertions which have attracted a good

---

[14] One may probably add a conviction that the human soul is immortal, on the basis both of his remarks at the end of the *Apology* (40C–42A), which admittedly contain an element of ambivalence, probably in deference to the range of beliefs within the jury, and of the comprehensive arguments in the *Phaedo*; but that does not imply any degree of certainty as to the nature of the soul's life after death.

[15] Presented at 87A as an 'hypothesis', such as geometers propose on occasion.

[16] I realise, of course, that this proposition precisely forms the subject of an *aporia* both at the end of the *Protagoras* and in the *Meno*, but I would venture to assert that Plato intends us to conclude that this is indeed a principle that Socrates lives by.

deal of attention, not least from Gregory Vlastos himself,[17] and which, it seems to me, could well have encouraged Carneades to propound his formula of various degrees of *pithanotês*. At 507C–D, in the course of a quite uncharacteristically long and impassioned speech, Socrates makes the following assertion:

> That, then, is the position I take (viz., that the temperate and good man will be supremely happy, and the intemperate and evil supremely unhappy), and I affirm it to be true, and if it is true, then the man who wishes to be happy must, it seems, pursue and practise temperance, and each of us must flee from indiscipline with all the speed in his power and contrive, preferably, to have no need of being disciplined, but if he or any of those belonging to him, whether individual or city, has need of it, then he must suffer punishment and be disciplined, if he is to be happy.[18]

The phrase translated 'this is the position I take' is *houtô tithemai*, that is to say: 'Such is my *thesis*', and Socrates declares this thesis to be true (*alêthê*). A little further along in this speech (508E–509A), he lays things on the line even more forcefully – before then seeming to row back significantly:

> These facts, which were shown to be such as I stated them some-time earlier in our previous discussion, are buckled fast and clamped together (*katekhetai kai dedetai*) – to put it somewhat crudely – by arguments of iron and adamant (*sidêrois kai adamantinois logois*) – at least so it would appear as matters stand. And unless you or one still more vigorous than yourself can undo them, it is impossible to speak aright except as I am now speaking. For what I say is always the same: *that I do not know how these things are* (*hoti egô tauta ouk oida hopôs ekhei*), but I do know that, of all whom I have ever met either before or now, no one who put forward another view has failed to make himself a laughing-stock (*katagelastos einai*).[19]

So what, one might ask – and many have asked! – is going on here? On the one hand, Socrates is absolutely convinced that he is right about his thesis; one can hardly improve on its being bound by *logoi*

[17] 'Socrates' Disavowal of Knowledge', in (1994), pp. 48–66; but cf. also (1991), p. 84.
[18] I borrow the translation of W.D. Woodhead, *Socratic Dialogues* (Edinburgh, 1963), lightly emended.
[19] *Ibid.*

of iron and adamant![20] But on the other hand, he disclaims *knowledge* of how things really are, and is prepared to envisage, albeit perhaps with a certain measure of irony, someone coming along even more vigorous – or how ever one might best render *neanikôteros*: perhaps 'more bumptious'? – than Callicles, who might contrive to dissolve these *logoi*. All he is sure of, as he says, is that he has never come across anyone, in all his years of practising the *elenchus*, who did not tie himself in knots, and become a laughing-stock (*katagelastos*), in trying to maintain the opposite thesis.

So, is this knowledge or is it not? Gregory Vlastos, it seems to me, has, in the essay just mentioned ('Socrates' Disavowal of Knowledge'), provided a most plausible formula for resolving this quandary – though I believe that it has not commended itself, perhaps inevitably, to all members of the tribe of philosophers.[21] Vlastos leads into his solution by presenting a rather effective illustration, as follows (p. 46):

> Consider the proposition, 'Very heavy smoking is a cause of cancer.' Ordinarily I would have no hesitation in saying that I know this, though I have not researched the subject and have not tried to learn even half of what could be learned from those who have. Now suppose that I am challenged, 'But *do* you know it?' Sensing the shift to the stronger criteria for 'knowing' the questioner has in view, I might then freely confess that I don't, adding perhaps, 'If you want to talk to someone who does, ask N.' – a renowned medical physiologist who has been researching the problem for years. By saying in this context, 'He knows, I don't,' I would not be implying that I had made a mistake when I had previously said I did know – that what I should have said instead is that all I had was a true belief. The conviction on whose strength I had acted when I gave up smoking years ago had not been just a true belief. I had reasons for it – imperfect ones, to be sure, which would not have been nearly good enough for a research scientist: in his case it would be a disgrace to say *he* knows on reasons no better than those. But for me

20 The phrase is somewhat reminiscent of the specification in the *Meno* (98A) of 'true opinions' (*doxai alêtheis*) needing to be 'bound down by the calculation of a reason'.
21 Alexander Nehamas, for one, who says (Nehamas (1998), p. 74): 'A central problem with this view is that the notion of a "philosophical" knowledge as Vlastos understands it is systematically articulated only in the middle and later writings of Plato and in the works of Aristotle.' True enough, perhaps, but it seems to me that this Vlastonian distinction is at least implicit in the *Gorgias* passages discussed here.

those reasons were, and still are, good enough 'for all practical purposes'; on the strength of those admittedly imperfect reasons I had made one of the *wisest* decisions of my life.

This delightfully personal testimony seems to me to set out the situation very well – with the modification, perhaps, that Vlastos' 'renowned medical physiologist' will be Socrates' god Apollo, or God in general, rather than any mortal expert. Vlastos wishes to emphasize that we are not here concerned with a distinction between 'knowledge' and 'belief (*pistis*), as set out, for example, at *Rep.* 5, 477E. His claim would be that, for all practical purposes, he *knows* – he does not just *believe* – that heavy smoking is very bad for you – and so, I submit, do all of us, including many of those who have not yet given up the weed! But we all, or most of us, readily admit that we are not fully acquainted with all of the technical details as to why nicotine does such dreadful things to our internal organs. And the same could be said of a wide range of facts about our everyday world which we 'know' for all practical purposes.[22]

So Vlastos proposes a distinction between knowledge of the most comprehensive type, which comprehends not only the given fact, but also the whole range of *reasons* which cause it to be the case, and a more provisional, but still thoroughly serviceable, level of knowledge, which results from years – or even a lifetime – of maintaining a given principle against all comers (this works primarily, it must be said, in the case of *ethical* principles) without meeting anyone who can confute one. He sets out the distinction as follows (*loc. cit.* pp. 55–6):

> I shall use 'knowledge$_C$' to designate knowledge so conceived (sc. a comprehensive knowledge of causes as well as facts) using the subscript as a reminder that infallible certainty was its hallmark. Now whatever Socrates might be willing to say he *knows* in the domain of ethics would have to be knowledge reached and tested through his own personal method of inquiry, the elenchus; this is his only method of searching for moral truth. So when he avows knowledge – as we have seen he does, rarely, but unmistakeably – the

---

[22] I would adduce, as one such instance, my 'knowledge' that human actions are responsible for global warming. I do not wish to say merely that I *believe* this, or that I *conjecture* it; I know it. But of course I am not an expert on the mechanics of climate change, so I do not know$_C$ *all* the whys and wherefores of this; I merely know of people who do.

content of that knowledge must be propositions he thinks elenctically justifiable. I shall therefore call it 'elenctic knowledge', abbreviating to 'knowledge$_E$'.

As I say, I find this a most useful distinction, even if it is not one ever made explicitly by Socrates himself in the dialogues. But my purpose here is not so much to defend it as a valid strategy for solving the conundrum of what degree of certainty Socrates actually attributed to the principles by which he lived, as to consider to what extent it might have influenced the position adopted by one of his more distinguished later followers, Carneades of Cyrene, head of the Academy in the latter half of the second century BCE.[23]

Carneades

We find quite an extensive account of Carneades' epistemology in Sextus Empiricus, *Against the Logicians* I (= *Against the Mathematicians* 7.159–189)[24], and I propose to base myself largely on that, though with due attention also to Cicero's *Academica* 2. We must recognize at the outset, of course, that all evidence as to the philosophical position maintained by Carneades (as would be the case for any member of the sceptical Academy) is fraught with uncertainty and the possibility of distortion, as, for one thing, he did not, as a matter of policy, commit his views to paper, and for another, the body of works which preserve his (probable) views, compiled by his faithful follower Clitomachus, have themselves not survived, and are being relayed to us by other sources, whether generally sympathetic, such as Cicero, or with something of an axe to grind, as is the case with Sextus. However, in the case of Sextus, one can at least be reasonably assured that he is not making

---

[23] The attempt by Arcesilaus, founder of the 'New Academy' to co-opt Socrates as a sceptic has been well discussed by A.A. Long (1988); while his effort to co-opt Plato in the same role has been argued for by Julia Annas (1992). Arcesilaus' position, however, insofar as we know it, seems to have been a good deal more absolute than that of Carneades, in the direction of 'suspension of judgement' (*epokhê*) and 'equipollence' (*isostheneia*); cf. Sextus, *AM* 7.150–8; Cicero, *Fin.* 2.2; *De Orat.* 3.67. See also the useful discussion by Richard Bett (1989).

[24] Also a summary account in *PH* 1.226–31, which transposes the two higher stages of *pithanotês*, and is in general less accurate. On Carneades' position in general, I am much indebted to the detailed discussion of James Allen (1994), though he does make rather heavy weather of the precise formulation of the three stages of probability! Such subtleties are, fortunately, not germane to my main thesis.

up the most distinctive features of Carneades' position out of the whole cloth, as he quite specifically makes use of technical vocabulary to describe the various levels of 'persuasiveness', or *pithanotês*, in the Carneadic scheme, and these are largely confirmed by evidence from Cicero.[25]

There is also the problem, presented to us by Cicero in the *Academica* (2.78; cf. also 139), that there was a dispute among Carneades' pupils as to whether he actually maintained the views that he propounded, or merely advanced them for the sake of argument; his pupil Metrodorus, the teacher of Philo of Larissa, maintained the former, while his chief pupil, and recorder of his opinions, Clitomachus maintained the latter – indeed Clitomachus is on record (*ap.* Cic. *Acad.* 2.139) as declaring that 'he had never been able to understand what Carneades did accept'. I think that we should go with Clitomachus on this one,[26] as I would discern here a good piece of evidence of Carneades' concern to maintain what he would have seen as a Socratic position: one may advance views of varying degrees of plausibility, but one always maintains the overall position that one cannot absolutely stand over anything (cf. *Gorg.* 509A: 'I do not know how these things are.').[27]

So, with these provisos, let us look at the text. We may note at the outset, however, a distinction of some significance between the respective fields in which Socrates and Carneades are applying their rules of persuasiveness: Socrates is concerned primarily with the field of ethical principles, not with ordinary cases of sensory perception;

---

[25] *Acad.* 1.99–104. There is, admittedly, the disquieting possibility that Sextus is actually deriving his information here, not directly from Clitomachus, but rather from the *Kanonika* of Antiochus of Ascalon, since Antiochus is suddenly quoted, on a detail of doctrine, at §162, and Antiochus would have an axe to grind as well; but once again, there is no reason here for Antiochus to be making up details of doctrine.

[26] Admittedly, Rudolf Hirzel, who first raised this question back in (1883), pp. 162–80, opts for Metrodorus, followed by most later authorities. Pierre Couissin (1923, pp. 104f.), however, opts for Clitomachus, and I would agree with him. A.A. Long has some useful remarks to make on this question in (1967), pp. 73–5, as does Bett (1989), pp. 83–90, and Thorsrud, in Bett (2010).

[27] He may also, it seems to me, have been influenced to some extent by Socrates' remarks at *Tht.* 150B–D, where he is describing his role as a midwife. It is at any rate interesting that the Anonymous Theaetetus Commentator (admittedly from a rather later period) interprets Socrates as saying here, when he declares that he is 'barren of wisdom', that the sort of wisdom he lacks is that which other people attribute to the great sophists, but which he himself would attribute to God alone (54.23–38).

Carneades, primarily because of his desire to counter the Stoics, is concerned rather with the criteria for persuasiveness in ordinary cases of sensory perception;[28] however, we may be permitted to assume, I think, that he extended these principles to the moral sphere – as, of course, did the Stoics.[29] At any rate, Sextus begins as follows (§159),[30] presenting Carneades as an uncompromising sceptic:

> His first line of argument, directed at all opponents alike (sc. not just the Stoics), is that by which he establishes that there is absolutely no criterion of truth – neither reason, nor sense-perception, nor mental presentation (*phantasia*), nor anything else that exists; for these things, one and all, play us false.

He backs up this position by a complex argument reported by Sextus in the following sections (§§160–5), which we fortunately need not dwell on in the present context,[31] but which involves insisting on the irreducibly subjective element in, first, sense-perception, then *phantasia*, and finally reason (*logos*), since it is dependent on the first two. This should establish Carneades as a thorough-going sceptic, but this is far from the whole story. Even a sceptical philosopher must conduct his life on certain principles, after all, and Carneades has a strategy for this.

Sextus continues (§166):[32]

> These were the arguments which Carneades set forth in detail, in his controversy with the other philosophers, to prove the non-existence of the criterion; yet, as he too finds himself solicited (*apaitoumenos*)[33]

---

[28] Indeed, it may be said that the Stoic theory of the cognitive impression throws down the gauntlet to the Platonist position that the fluidity of objects in the physical world and the imperfection of our sense-organs make certainty at the physical level impossible, thus forcing the Platonists to meet them on this field of play.

[29] Gisela Striker makes this point well in (1996), p. 107.

[30] I borrow the Loeb translation of Bury, modified.

[31] Although we may note the probable dependence of Carneades' assertion of the need for the *aisthêsis* to be set into motion by an external stimulus, and thus being only really operative as a sense-organ when it is 'disturbed' through being presented by something 'evident' (*enarges*), on Socrates' exposition of the 'Protagorean' position in *Tht.* 153B–154B. The fact that it would seem to us that Socrates is giving a distinctly ironic account of a whole array of previous philosophers, 'with Homer as its captain' (153a2), need not deter the New Academics from taking this as a Socratic doctrine.

[32] I borrow the Loeb translation of Bury, modified.

[33] 'Solicited by whom?', one might ask. Sextus (who may here, in fact, be reproducing Antiochus) may mean 'by the Stoics', 'by his own pupils', or even by Reason itself. One may easily imagine, at any rate, that Carneades felt some pressure to provide a formula

for a criterion for the conduct of life and for the attainment of happiness, he is practically (*dynamei*) compelled on his own account to frame a theory about it.

And Sextus now proceeds to set this out (§§167ff.).[34] What we find is an ascending series of three degrees of *pithanotês*, consisting of (a) the basic *pithanê phantasia*, or 'persuasive presentation'; (b) the presentation that is 'persuasive and not contradicted' (*pithanê kai aperispastos*) and (c) the presentation that is not just persuasive and not contradicted, but 'thoroughly checked out' (*pithanê kai aperispastos kai diexôdeumenê*) – this last verb signifying something like 'going right through', or 'inspection from every angle'.

Before, however, Sextus turns to the discussion of these, he introduces a significant feature of Carneades' theory:

> The presentation, then, is a presentation of something (*tinos phantasia*) – namely, both of that *from which* it comes and that *in which* it occurs; that from which it comes being, let us say, the externally existent sensible object, and that in which it occurs being, for instance, a man. And such being its nature, it will have two aspects (*skheseis*), one in its relation to the object presented (*to phantaston*), the second in its relation to the subject experiencing the presentation (*ho phantasioumenos*).
>
> Now in regard to its aspect in relation to the object presented it is either true or false – true when it is in accord with the object presented, but false when it is not in accord. But in regard to its aspect in relation to the subject experiencing the presentation, the one kind of presentation is apparently true, the other apparently false; and of these the apparently true is termed by the Academics 'impression' (*emphasis*) and 'persuasiveness' (*pithanotês*) and 'persuasive presentation'; while the not apparently true is denominated 'mis-impression' (*apemphasis*)[35] and 'unconvincing and unpersuasive presentation' (*apeithês kai apithanos phantasia*); for neither that which appears false, nor that which, though true, does not appear so to us, is naturally convincing to us.

according to which one could live. Bett discusses this briefly, in an appendix to his article (1989), pp. 93–4.

[34] The tone of Sextus' remarks here could simply reflect his own attitude – he does not, after all, regard Carneades as being a true sceptic, since he does not regard Academics as true sceptics; but the tone could also be borrowed from Antiochus, in whose interest it would be to show that force of circumstances compelled Carneades to advance a long way towards (at least modified) certainty.

[35] This is a notable technicality. The word has a 'normal' meaning of 'misleading' or 'confusing impression', as e.g. in Strabo, *Geogr.* 10.2.12, which would approximate to what is meant here, namely, a sense-datum that contains some obscure or misleading aspect.

This account, though somewhat peculiar, has much of interest. It is odd, perhaps, to distinguish two sources of unclarity in an act of perception, the objective and the subjective. Surely, one might think, if a given sense-perception is obscure, it is the fault of the perceiving organ (defective eyesight or hearing), or its situation (too far away, light too dim); the object is what it is. But this is not necessarily so. One may have objects that are naturally obscure (a venomous toad that looks like a stone, perhaps) or deliberately deceptive (*tromp l'oeil* effects, wax fruit, and so on). In fact, I would discern here an influence, whether remote or direct, from that passage of the *Theaetetus* (156A–157B), a continuation of that mentioned above (n. 20), where Socrates is (rather tendentiously) setting out a 'Protagorean' theory of sense-perception, involving states of flux on the part of both subject and object, as they come together momentarily to produce a sensation. It may seem obvious to us that Socrates is being ironic here, but it was not obvious to young Theaetetus, and it may well not have been obvious to the Platonists of the New Academy.

At any rate, we have here the possible sources of unpersuasiveness in impressions equally divided between subject and object. Carneades' purpose in making these distinctions, as emerges in what follows (§§169–72), is to exclude as *kritēria* all sense-impressions that exhibit any degree of deceptiveness or obscurity, arising either from the subject or the object. We are left, then, with 'that which is manifestly true and provides a sufficiently clear impression' to serve as our *kritērion*.[36] But within this broad definition, as it emerges, there are various degrees of plausibility, as follows.

First of all, it seems (§176), Carneades made the point that no presentation (*phantasia*) is isolated from others, but they come linked together in a kind of chain (*halyseōs tropon*), and these other *phantasiai* may either reinforce, or at least not contradict, the original one,

---

[36] It is worth noting, I think, in this connection that the second-century CE Neopythagoreanizing Platonist Numenius of Apamea – no friend of the sceptical New Academy – in his treatise *On the Unfaithfulness of the Academy to Plato* (Fr. 26, 103–111 Des Places) reports that Carneades distinguished between the 'ungraspable' (*akatalēpton*) and the 'unclear' (*adēlon*), asserting that, while nothing is 'graspable', in the Stoic sense, not all things were unclear. States of affairs that are 'clear' would presumably correspond to the highest degree of the 'plausible'.

clear and plausible as it may have been, or they may go against it. If the former is the case, we move up to the next stage of plausibility, the 'persuasive and non-contradicted' (*pithanê kai aperispastos*):

> So whenever none of these presentations disturbs our faith by appearing false, but all with one accord appear true, our belief is the greater. For we believe that this man is Socrates from the fact he possesses all his customary qualities – colour, size, shape, conversation, dress, and his position in a place where there is no one exactly like him. (§§177–8)

If we try to conjure up a real situation,[37] let us suppose that we observe, from the other side of the street, our friend Socrates emerging from a pub that we know that he does not normally frequent – let us say, Whelan's on Wexford Street (in Dublin) – whereas we know him to be a habitué of O'Neill's in Andrew Street.[38] So we look again, closely. And now, as we focus more carefully, either we observe that after all it is *not* Socrates: the hair is slightly wrong, the walk is slightly wrong, this figure is a bit taller, nose not quite so snub; or, conversely, we are confirmed in our original impression: it *is* after all very like Socrates. So we cross the road to confront him, and find that, after all, the walk, the talk, the nose, the dress are all correct.

We are now, I should say, at the *aperispastos* stage. All the subsidiary *phantasiai* look good, the light is favourable, and one's own sense-faculties seem to be in good working order. But we could still be faced with a very clever and accomplished Socrates-impersonator, intent on sowing confusion among Socrates' friends and admirers. What we now need is some background information as to why Socrates is found emerging from Whelan's instead of propping up the bar, or holding court in his favourite corner, in O'Neill's. And that is why we probe for background information. We now learn from him that he was drawn away from his usual haunts down to

---

[37] Ancient critics, as represented by Sextus (*AM* 7.253–7) preferred to adduce mythological examples, viz. Admetus demurring at the clear presentation of his wife Alcestis, when brought back from Hades to him by Heracles, and Menelaus, similarly demurring at the clear presentation of Helen in front of him when he reached Egypt on his journey home; but I prefer to adduce a 'real life' example.

[38] I venture, for the purpose, to transpose Socrates to contemporary Dublin; the reader can make appropriate adjustments. O'Neill's is a respectable pub in the vicinity of Trinity College, much frequented by certain of the faculty; Whelan's is a somewhat sleazy bar in another quarter of the city, frequented by the younger set, and hosting performances of popular music.

Whelan's to meet a fellow who was alleged to hold interesting views on moral questions, and that he had just finished having a stimulating conversation with him on the nature of justice, which had only just been broken off because this chap suddenly remembered that he had another urgent engagement, and had hurried off.

Now that we have fully probed the background to this unexpected presentation, we have arrived, I would suggest, at a *phantasia* which is 'thoroughly checked-out' (*diexôdeuomenê*), and that, Carneades suggests to us, is as far as we need to go for the purpose of living a coherent and rational life: we have no need of Stoic *katalêpsis*, which is not attainable by ordinary mortals anyway.

Sextus gives the following description of this final stage (§§181–2):

> Still more trustworthy than the irreversible presentation, and yielding a level of judgement that is supremely perfect (*teleiotatên poiousa tên krisin*), is that which, in addition to being irreversible, is also thoroughly checked out. What the distinctive feature of this is we must next explain. Now in the case of the irreversible presentation it is merely required that none of the presentations in the concurrence should disturb (*perispân*) us by a suspicion of its falsity, but all should be manifestly true and not implausible; but in the case of the concurrence (*syndromê*) which involves the 'checked-out' presentation, we scrutinize attentively each of the presentations in the concurrence – just as is the practice at meetings of the assembly (*ekklêsia*), when the people (*dêmos*) makes inquiry about each of those who desire to be magistrates or judges, to see whether he is worthy to be entrusted with the magistracy or the judgeship.

With the help of this effective example – drawn, interestingly, from the practice of Classical Athens, the *dokimasia* of incoming magistrates, which was indeed a searching process, rather than from anything that Sextus could have met with, I think, in the Roman Empire of the second century CE – Sextus reinforces his characterization of the highest stage of the Carneadic criterion. One of the examples that he adduces (§§186–8; cf. also *PH* 1.227–8), which seems to go back to the New Academicians themselves, is that of the coil of rope in the darkened room, which we may adduce to supplement that of Socrates coming out of the wrong pub.

The scenario is that 'on seeing a coil of rope in a darkened room, a man jumps over it, conceiving it for the moment to be a snake, but turning back afterwards he enquires into the truth, and on finding it motionless, he is already inclined to think that it is not a snake' (this we may take to represent the basic *pithanê phantasia*), 'but, as he reckons, all the same, that snakes too are motionless at times, when numbed by winter's frost,[39] he prods at the coiled mass with a stick, and then, after thus testing (*ekperiodeusas*) the presentation received, he assents to the fact that it is false to suppose that the body presented to him is a snake'.

Here in fact the two higher stages of raising the plausibility of the presentation seem rather to be conflated by Sextus, and might be unpacked as follows: first, one pokes at the coiled mass, and gets no reaction; then, perhaps, one goes and gets a lantern (as one should have done in the first place!), and takes a good look at it, before picking it up and putting it on a shelf.

And indeed it is just such procedures of looking, checking, and then reassuring ourselves by further supplementary actions that make up much of our daily existence, without ever attaining to the certainties of the Stoic Sage.

Conclusion

But we have dwelt long enough, perhaps, on the details of Carneades' proposals for a serviceable criterion. Let us return to the reason that I have focused on this aspect of his thought. Carneades, we must recall, is concerned to counter the challenge of the Stoics, and of Chrysippus in particular, that refusal of assent (*synkatathesis*) – since it is impossible, as they would argue, to have an impulse (*hormê*) towards something without assenting to its actuality, or to the truth of a proposition about it – must lead to total inactivity (*apraxia*). His response to this[40] is to propound, *as a thesis,* a schema of three ascending levels of *pithanotês* which may serve as a non-dogmatic criterion for living. I emphasize 'as a thesis', as I would hold, as I remarked earlier, to the tradition passed down by Clitomachus, rather than that attributed to Metrodorus, that Carneades advanced his philosophical positions always 'dialectically', never committing himself to them absolutely, so as to preserve his sceptical stance (cf. Cic. *Acad.* 2.78: *magis disputatum quam probatum*).

---

[39] I.e. it may be hibernating.
[40] Well discussed by Gisela Striker in 1980/1996, pp. 105–15.

This position is dramatized most forcefully in the famous incident that took place during his service on an embassy from Athens to Rome in 155 BCE, recounted by Cicero in *Rep.* 3.9, where Carneades argued with equal force and ingenuity in favour of and against justice on consecutive days – thus deeply shocking his Roman audience, who had been much impressed by the first speech!

My thesis here is that Carneades is able, in adopting the stance that he did, that is to say, being prepared to propound a high degree of belief in selected presentations (what one might venture to equate with Vlastos' 'Knowledge$_E$'), on this basis to conduct his life rationally and attain happiness (*eudaimonia*), while holding himself aloof, at one remove from his interlocutors, to such a degree that his most faithful pupil and recorder, Clitomachus, can assert, as we have seen, that he was never at any stage of his association with him certain as to what his Master believed. Even so did Socrates seem to tease and baffle Plato and his other followers – though Plato's reaction is to get his own back by creating, with brilliant literary artistry, a semi-fictional 'Socrates'-figure who can be made to say, at various stages of Plato's own philosophical development, whatever Plato wants him to say.

We have here an interesting parallelism: Socrates has his recorder and interpreter, Plato, from whose brilliant portrayals of his Master, happily preserved to us in full, Carneades, and we ourselves, including Gregory Vlastos, can derive what conclusions we wish about Socrates' true beliefs; and Carneades in turn has his recorder, the faithful Clitomachus – 'pretty smart', remarks Cicero rather snidely (*Acad.* 2.98), 'as being a Carthaginian' (*homo et acutus, ut Poenus, et valde studiosus ac diligens*) – whose works – four books of 'memorabilia', it would seem (*ibid.* 99) – are unfortunately lost to us, but of which we can recover something from Cicero and from Sextus. I would suggest that, from a combination of the passages that I quoted at the outset, especially those from the *Apology* and the *Gorgias*, Carneades was able to derive a stance that preserved a balance between Stoic dogmatism and total *epokhê*, thus enabling him, in Myles Burnyeat's phrase, to 'live his scepticism', while contriving to baffle his immediate followers, as well as, of course, ourselves.

CHAPTER 6

Plutarch's Relation to the New-Academic Tradition

Having in the previous chapter examined the philosophical position of a prominent member of the sceptical 'New-Academic' wing of Platonism, it seems appropriate to close by considering an example of constructive engagement with this aspect of the Platonist tradition, on the part of at least one prominent figure from the later 'Middle Platonic' period, with a view to including it within the broader spectrum of Platonism.

Within this tradition, the Platonist Plutarch of Chaeroneia would not normally be regarded as being particularly close to the sceptical or aporetic wing or tendency, but – as Jan Opsomer has well pointed out in his most useful book *In Search of the Truth*[1] – that impression would not be entirely correct. For one thing, despite his own adherence to positive dogma, Plutarch is one of the few later Platonists who persist in regarding the philosophers of the New Academy as an integral part of the Platonic tradition, and he likes to strike sceptical attitudes, particularly when engaging in polemic with the Stoics, and, to some extent, with the Epicureans.[2] The existence of a work, *On the Unity of the Academy from Plato* – now sadly lost, but attested in the Catalogue of Lamprias (no. 63) – testifies to this tendency of his, and stands in sharp contrast to the strong attack on the sceptical Academy launched later in the second century by the Neopythagoreanizing Platonist

---

[1] (1998). I shall be much indebted to this excellent study in what follows. A useful discussion also can be found in Brittain (2007).

[2] I have been fairly reprimanded by Daniel Babut ((2007), p. 67 n.17) for in the past rather dismissing Plutarch's New-Academic sympathies, as follows (Dillon (1999), p. 305): 'As for the New Academy, despite his retention of some Academic sceptic traits as weapons against the Stoa, he reveals no affinity for such figures as Arcesilaus and Carneades.' I would certainly modify that view now, on maturer consideration, without wishing to retract it entirely!

Numenius of Apamea, in his work *On the Divergence of the Academics from Plato* (Frr. 24–6 Des Places).

Indeed, even Plutarch's composition of dialogues, starting as they each do from an *aporia* of one sort or another (e.g. 'What is the meaning of the E at Delphi?' (*On the E in Delphi*); 'What is the reason for the decline of oracles?' (*The Decline of Oracles*); 'What was the nature of Socrates' *daimonion?*' (*On the Daimonion of Socrates*); 'What is the reason for the face that appears on the Moon?' (*On the Face in the Moon*) – leading to the more general question 'What is the substance of the Moon?'), can also be seen as a manifestation of this tendency. He shows a deep interest in, and sympathy for, the personality of Socrates, and of his peculiar mode of philosophizing, both in his dialogue *On the Daimonion of Socrates* and in the first *Platonic Question*, which involves an examination of the rationale behind Socratic 'midwifery'.

However, it must be admitted that, despite his reverence for Socrates (which provides a continuity with that which animated the leaders of the New-Academic tradition, such as Arcesilaus and Carneades), for Plutarch, an *aporia* – as particularly evidenced by the nine books of *Symposiac Questions*, as well as the volume of *Questions about Nature* (*problêmata physika*) – is more in the tradition of the Aristotelian *problêma* than of properly Socratic aporetic questioning, as practised by the New Academy.[3]

A good place to start our investigation, I think, would be the rather programmatic first *zêtêma* of his collection of *Platonic Questions*, which proposes the question, arising from a passage which obviously much affected the New Academicians, *Tht.* 149A–151D: 'Why ever did the god, as stated in the *Theaetetus* (150c7–8), bid Socrates act as midwife to others, but prevent him from himself begetting?' This passage had already been dealt with by the Anonymous Theaetetus Commentator (cols. 49–56) – where the Anon., it must be said, is rather more concerned than Plutarch to counter the New Academic embracing of Socrates as a true sceptic; Plutarch, on the other hand,

---

[3] The distinction between the Platonic and Aristotelian uses of *aporia* is nicely brought out by Gareth Mathews (1999) in his penultimate chapter (11), pp. 109ff. For Aristotle, in general, an *aporia* is not an occasion for existential perplexity, but rather a particular problem to be solved by further research.

is prepared to accept Socrates' declaration of ignorance as quite free of irony and fooling,[4] He also feels the need to defend Socrates' apparently arrogant comparison of himself to a god (151C5–D3):[5]

> For a great many men, my excellent friend, have got into such a state of mind towards me as practically to bite when I remove some silliness of theirs; and they do not believe that I am doing this out of benevolence, for they are a long way from knowing that *no god is malevolent towards men, and that neither do I do any such deed out of malevolence,* but that it is quite illicit for me to admit falsehood and suppress truth.

To take this latter passage first, it would seem to me probable that Plato intends Socrates to mean merely that he is acting as the servant of God (or more specifically, of the god Apollo),[6] and that the god would not have commissioned him to do any evil to his fellow-men, but this solution (which itself leaves Socrates sounding somewhat pompous) does not seem to have occurred to any ancient commentator. Plutarch, in attempting to defend Socrates against a charge of pomposity and 'talking big' (*megalêgoria*), such as was levelled at him happily by Epicureans such as Colotes, offers the solution that Socrates is really just referring to his own intellect, as the highest part of himself, which is characterized by Plato, at the end of the *Timaeus* (90A) as a *daimôn* given to each of us by God – though Plutarch here instead quotes Menander ('for our intelligence is god', Fr. 762 Kock) and Heraclitus ('The character of a man is his *daimôn*,' Fr. B114 D–K).

As to the former, and primary, point, Plutarch, after explaining (999E–F) that Socrates saw it as his mission to rescue young men from the clutches of the Sophists, who were filling them with self-conceit (*oiêma*) and sham-wisdom (*doxosophia*), and encouraging them to futile disputatiousness, by introducing his *elenchus* like a purgative

---

[4] 'For he would not have invoked the god's name in a spirit of irony or foolery' – with a reference to Alcibiades' remarks at *Symp.* 216E4–5.

[5] I borrow the Loeb translation of Cherniss & Helmbold, *Moralia* 12 (Cambridge, MA, 1927).

[6] Modern commentators, at least in the English-speaking world, are strangely unconcerned about the meaning of this remark. Cornford (1935), McDowell (1973), and Burnyeat, in his introduction to M.J. Levett, (1990), make no mention of it. Only Lewis Campbell in his edition (1883) offers a rather coy interpretation, supposing that Socrates is referring to 'the presiding genius of his Art' – by which he may mean his *daimonion,* but that is not clear. I fear, however, that I have not made a comprehensive check of editions.

medicine (*kathartikon pharmakon*), goes on to explain why this calls for the suppression, or even the effective absence, of any partisan views of one's own (1000A):[7]

> In the second place, while the exercise of judgement is beneficial, begetting (sc. of doctrines) is an obstacle to it, for what loves is blinded about the thing it loves,[8] and nothing of one's own is so beloved as is an opinion or an argument by its parent. For the distribution of offspring that is proverbially[9] most just is most unjust when applied to arguments, for in the former case one must take what is one's own, but in the latter what is best, even it be another's. For this reason, the man who begets his own becomes a poorer judge of others.

His argument here would suit either the more properly Sceptic view of Socrates as claiming to know nothing, or the more broadly Platonist view of Socrates as holding back on his opinions for pedagogical reasons. From what follows, however, it appears that Plutarch is more inclined to the Sceptic position. He adduces the comparison of someone whose hearing is obstructed by internal ringing and buzzing (a sort of tinnitus, one might say) with one whose judgement is obstructed by the possession of doctrines to which he is devoted; he simply cannot give a fair hearing to other points of view (1000B–C). He continues (1000C):

> Furthermore, if nothing is apprehensible (*katalêpton*) and knowable to man, it was reasonable for God to have prevented Socrates from begetting inane and false and baseless notions and to compel him to refute (*elengkhein*) the others who were forming such opinions. For the discourse that liberates from the greatest of evils, deception and vanity, was not a slight but a very great help –
>
> > the gift God didn't grant even to the sons of Asclepius (*Theog.* 432).
>
> For the treatment given by Socrates was not of the body, but was a purgation of the ulcerous and corrupted soul.

Plutarch here plainly has in mind (as duly noted by Cherniss *ad loc.*) such a passage as *Soph.* 230C–231B where the Visitor from Elea is

---

[7] I borrow the Loeb translation of Cherniss & Helmbold, *Moralia* 12 (Cambridge, MA, 1927).

[8] A creative application of a dictum from Plato's *Laws* 5, 731E, where Plato is exploring the causes of crime, as rooted in selfishness.

[9] No relevant proverb seems to be elsewhere attested, but it must, I think, have concerned the selection of one's own offspring by parents in some situation.

commending the method of *elenchus* as the best purgative of the corrupted soul. Interestingly, though, after all this emphasis on Socrates' freedom from opinions of his own, Plutarch ends his first Platonic Question by asserting that Socrates' real purpose in subjecting young men to the *elenchus* was not simply to reduce them to perplexity, but rather to provoke in them a reminiscence (*anamnêsis*) of true reality, of which they have innate conceptions (1000D–E):

> Consider too that, while the other things, poetry and mathematics and rhetorical speeches and sophistic doctrines, which the *daimonion* prevented Socrates from begetting, were worth no serious concern, what Socrates held to be alone wisdom, that which he called 'passion for the divine and intelligible',[10] is for human beings a matter not of generation or of discovery, but of reminiscence. For this reason Socrates was not engaged in teaching anything, but by exciting perplexities (*aporiai*) as if inducing the inception of labour-pains in young men, he would arouse and quicken and help to deliver their innate conceptions (*emphytoi noêseis*);[11] and his name for this was obstetric skill (*maiôtikê tekhnê*), since it does not, as other men pretended to do, implant in those who come upon it intelligence from without, but shows that they have it native within themselves, but undeveloped and confused and in need of nurture and stabilization.

The upshot of this whole *zêtêma*, then, would seem to be to situate Socrates judiciously within the Platonic tradition, recognizing on the one hand both the genuineness of his claim to 'know nothing', at least of those areas of expertise professed by sophists and other 'experts', and on the other his concern, by proper maieutic procedures, to lead his interlocutors to the 'recollection' of Forms, or the activation of their 'innate concepts'. In one respect, therefore, his claim to 'know nothing' is straightforward, and has two aspects: (a) his abjuring of any expertise in what one might term 'science and

---

[10] A reference here to Diotima's description of the culmination of the ascent to the Beautiful in the *Symposium* (210E–212A), combined with a glancing allusion to the description of the wisdom of the Guardians in *Rep.* 4, 429A.

[11] An interesting employment here of an essentially Stoic concept, the *koinai ennoiai*, or 'common concepts', but overlaid with a distinctively Platonic element: the capacity for receiving these *noêseis* is innate, but their source is independently existing Platonic Forms. Plutarch is by no means alone here, within the spectrum of Middle Platonism: Alcinous presents a very similar position in *Did.* ch. 4, 6.

technology', such as professed by sophists, and (b) his belief that knowledge in the fullest sense (that is, a complete comprehension of the causes and effects of everything) belongs to God alone; while, on the other hand, his claim of ignorance can be seen as a maieutic strategy, the holding back of any views of his own, primarily on moral questions, in order to draw out, through the *elenchus,* the concepts inhering in his interlocutors.[12]

This, then, constitutes one good instance of Plutarch's attitude to the aporetic aspect of his Platonic heritage. I propose to focus on just two others. First, as I have remarked earlier, one may expect to find Plutarch at his most aporetic when attacking one or other of his two main bugbears, the Stoics or the Epicureans – in either case, largely because of their attacks on the sceptical Academy of Arcesilaus and Carneades.[13] Of the five treatises in question, two against the Stoics (*On the Contradictions of the Stoics; On Common Notions, against the Stoics*)[14] and three against the Epicureans (*That a Pleasant Life is Impossible on the Principles of Epicurus; Is 'Live Unknown' a Wise Precept?; Against Colotes, on behalf of the Other Philosophers*), I will select some passages from the last one, since here Plutarch deals explicitly with Socrates (1116E–1119C), as part of a long list of earlier philosophers, starting with Democritus, whom Colotes has attacked.

Colotes' primary target was in fact his contemporary Arcesilaus,[15] but, for the purpose of undermining Arcesilaus' position, he chooses to place him in a sequence of philosophers who denied the possibility of knowledge, among whom is Socrates. In his polemic, Colotes is adopting a version of the Stoic imputation against Arcesilaus of *apraxia,* the impossibility for the sceptic, if he withholds assent to impressions, of acting at all – at least in any rational or consistent way. Why should he not eat grass instead of bread? Why, when he goes to eat, should he not try to stuff the food into his ear rather than

---

[12] The suggestion that Socrates has a concept of intelligible reality, we may note, is also made by Plutarch at *Adv. Col.* 1114C.

[13] Mauro Bonazzi (2003) has a useful discussion of Plutarch's attitude to Arcesilaus, on pp. 219–32.

[14] The summary of a third one exists: *That the Stoics make more paradoxical utterances than the poets.*

[15] Colotes of Lampsacus, a favoured pupil of Epicurus, seems to have composed this work in the 260s BCE.

his mouth? Why should he not try to exit a room by walking through the wall rather than the door? Why, when he wishes to bathe, should he not head for the mountain rather than the baths?

These gibes may have had some force against anyone maintaining total scepticism, as Arcesilaus appears to have done (though possibly only for polemical anti-Stoic purposes), but Plutarch, as becomes plain, is operating on the basis rather of the nuanced sceptical stance of Carneades, where one may act on the basis of perceived degrees of probability,[16] though without ever conceding the possibility of Stoic *katalêpsis*. Plutarch, admittedly, nowhere sets out the elaborate three-stage scale of plausibility that Carneades seems to have propounded, but it is pretty clear that it is Carneades' position that he is adopting.[17] After some brisk satirical ripostes to Colotes, he comes out with the following (1118B):[18]

> For it is only in doctrine and argument that these sages have the advantage over the rest of us;[19] to perceive with the senses and to receive impressions when confronted with appearances happens to everyone, since it is the work of causes that have nothing to do with reasoning. The inductive argument by which we conclude that the senses are not accurate or trustworthy does not deny that an object presents to us a certain appearance, but forbids us, though we continue to make use of the senses and take the appearance as our guide in what we do, to trust them as entirely and infallibly true. For we ask no more of them than utilitarian service in the unavoidable essentials, since there is nothing better available; but they do not provide perfect knowledge and understanding of a thing that the philosophical soul longs to acquire.

This, it seems to me, serves as a very good statement of at least the Carneadic position, which Plutarch seems to endorse. We do not have

---

[16] For the fullest account of Carneades' three stages of *pithanotês*, or 'plausibility', discussed in the previous chapter, see Sextus Empiricus, *AM* 7.159–89. One moves from a basic *pithanê phantasia* to one that 'plausible and uncontradicted (*pithanê kai adiaspastos*), and ultimately to one that is all that, but also 'thoroughly checked-out (*diexôduemenê*)'. On the basis of this last, one can act with virtual certainty, without, however, conceding anything to the Stoics.

[17] An alternative would be that he is adopting the position of Philo of Larissa, the pupil of his pupil Metrodorus, and last head of the sceptical Academy. I do not rule this out, but I feel that Carneades' position will do very well.

[18] I borrow the Loeb translation of Einarson & De Lacy, *Moralia* 7 (Cambridge, MA, 1927).

[19] He has just mentioned the *dogma* of Epicurus that 'no one but the sage (*sophos*) is unalterably convinced of anything' (1117F–Fr. 222 Usener).

to regard the senses as absolutely accurate or trustworthy in order to make use of them as our guide in day-to-day living, without taking them to be 'entirely and infallibly true'. The very last sentence, however, recalls us to the fact that there is, after all, a realm of true being, knowledge and understanding (*epistêmê kai gnôsis*) of which can be attained by the use of the mind, not the senses. We have no evidence that Plutarch subscribed to the pious rumour, possibly already promulgated by Philo of Larissa,[20] but firmly attested both by Numenius (Fr. 25. 75–83) and by Sextus Empiricus (*PH* 1.234), that Arcesilaus had only practised scepticism as a polemical tool against the Stoics, and to test the acumen of his students, while 'dogmatizing' in private, but his emphasis on Socrates' desire to stimulate *anamnesis* in his students seems to contain a suggestion of this theory, or at least to be compatible with it.

However that may be, Plutarch, after dealing briefly with the Megarian Stilpo, turns (1121Eff.) to a defence of Arcesilaus himself, who has been the real object of Colotes' whole tirade. Significantly, Plutarch, having accused Colotes of projecting back Arcesilaus' maintenance of *epokhê* onto, not only Socrates and Plato, but also such figures as Parmenides and Heraclitus, is quite prepared to accept that Arcesilaus would have been justified in this (1122A). The issue, after all, concerns the perception of the physical world, as to the uncertainties of which Plato is on the side of his sceptical followers. One may adduce, for instance, such a passage as *Phd.* 65A–B, where Socrates says to Simmias:

> 'Now take the acquisition of knowledge (*phronêsis*). Is the body a hindrance or not, if one takes it into partnership to share an investigation? What I mean is this. Is there any certainty in human sight and hearing, or is it true, as the poets are always dinning into our ears, that we neither hear nor see anything accurately? Yet if these senses are not clear or accurate, the rest can hardly be so, because they are all inferior to the first two. Don't you agree?'
> 'Certainly.'

Such a passage can be connected with, for example, Socrates' exposition of the 'Protagorean' theory of perception in the *Theaetetus* to

---

[20] Augustine, in his *Contra Academicos* (3. 20. 43) attributes this rumour to Cicero, in a lost part of his *Academica* (Fr. 210 Plasberg), which puts it back to the early first century BCE. It is hard to see who else Cicero could have picked this up from than Philo.

support a thoroughly 'sceptical' position on the accuracy of sensory perceptions. What Plutarch is concerned to counter here, however, is the Stoic and Epicurean gibe of *apraxia*, levelled, 'like the raising of a Gorgon's head' (1122B), against Arcesilaus' position. There is no reason, he argues, to suppose that impulse (*hormê*), without which action could not take place, requires 'assent' (*synkatathesis*), in anything like the Stoic sense:

> The soul has three motive forces (*kinêmata*): sensation, impulse, and assent. Now the movement of sensation cannot be eliminated, even if we wanted to; instead, upon encountering an object, we necessarily receive an imprint and are affected. Impulse, aroused by sensation, moves us in the shape of actions directed to suitable goals (*pros ta oikeia*):[21] a kind of casting weight (*rhopê*) has been put in the scale of our governing part (*hêgemonikon*), and a directed movement (*neusis*) is set afoot. So those who suspend judgement about everything do not eliminate this second movement either, but follow their impulse, which leads them to the suitable apparent object (*pros to phainomenon oikeion*).
>
> Then what is the only thing they avoid? That only in which falsity and error can arise, namely forming an opinion (*doxazein*) and thus falling rashly into assent (*synkatathesis*), although such an assent is a yielding to appearance that is due to weakness and is of no use whatever.[22] For two things are requisite for action (*praxis*): a presentation (*phantasia*) of something suitable, and an impulse towards the suitable object thus presented to appearance – neither of which conflicts with suspension of judgement (*epokhê*). For it is opinion (*doxa*) that the argument relieves us from, not impulse or sensation. So once some suitable object is perceived, no opinion is required to set us moving and keep us going in its direction; the impulse comes directly, and is a movement initiated and pursued by the soul.[23]

Plutarch thus appears to identify himself firmly with the position of Arcesilaus, as interpreted by himself, and to claim that position

---

[21] If Plutarch is reporting Arcesilaus accurately here, he would appear to be using a Stoic technical term for his own purposes. The term *oikeion*, which may be rendered 'suitable' or 'akin' to us, occurs repeatedly throughout this passage, as an equivalent for 'good' (*agathon*).

[22] Again, Plutarch/Arcesilaus would appear to be turning Stoic terminology against themselves: for Zeno (*SVF* 1. 67–9), opinion is 'weak' or 'false' assent; for Arcesilaus here, all assent is a result of 'weakness' (*astheneia*).

[23] I borrow the Loeb translation of Einarson & De Lacy, *Moralia* 7 (Cambridge, MA, 1927), slightly altered.

essentially for Plato and for Socrates – with the proviso, of course, that this relates exclusively to the physical world; our knowledge of the Forms, the contents of the intelligible world, is sourced quite differently. He proceeds to defend the New Academy for many pages more, revealing in the process, I would suggest, a good deal of the contents of his lost treatise, mentioned above, *On the Unity of the Academy from Plato*. It is interesting, for instance, that he can embrace the acceptance of such things as traditional religious practices and belief in oracles, which would certainly have been endorsed by Plato and Socrates (despite their attacks on unsuitable popular beliefs about the gods), within the ambit of Academic scepticism (1125Dff.). His rationale for this presumably is that such phenomena as religious practices, since they are endorsed by countless generations of men, fulfil the (Carneadic) condition of being 'thoroughly investigated (*diexôdeumenê*)', and thus merit the highest level of assent to their plausibility. At any rate, on religion he comes out with the following (1125DE):

> In your travels you may come upon cities without walls, writing, king, houses or property, doing without currency, having no notion of a theatre or gymnasium; but a city without holy places and gods, without any observance of prayers, oaths, oracles, sacrifices for blessings received or rites to avert evil, no traveller has seen or will ever see. No, I think a city might rather be formed without the ground it stands on than a government, once you remove all religion from under it, get itself established or, once established, survive.

Oddly, he here concords with the Stoic argument advanced by Chrysippus for the existence of gods, from the observation that all known nations and tribes believe in them, but the argument works just as well within the framework of Carneadic levels of plausibility – whatever about Arcesilaus' own position.

We may observe here, then, the lineaments of a Plutarchan Platonism that incorporates a moderate, or modulated, degree of scepticism, embracing the tradition of the New Academy. This sceptical tendency seems primarily to emerge, it must be said, in the context of combating the Stoics and Epicureans, but it can surface in interesting ways within Plutarch's non-polemical works.

I propose to end this chapter with a study of a rather curious and entertaining work, Plutarch's essay *On the Principle of Cold*.[24]

This short treatise, dedicated to his pupil Favorinus of Arles, who himself professed to be a follower of the sceptical Academy,[25] is a somewhat enigmatic document, but gains considerably in stature and interest, I think, if one regards it as essentially a light-hearted *jeu d'esprit*, designed both to salute, and (in a friendly spirit) to tease, Favorinus.

The topic is broached, initially, as an (Aristotelian-style) *aporia* or *problêma*: 'Is there an active principle (*dynamis*) of Cold, as there is of Heat (in the form of fire), through the presence (*parousia*) of which, and through participation (*metokhê*) in which, everything else becomes cold? Or is coldness rather a negation (*sterêsis*) of warmth, as they say darkness is of light, and rest of motion?'

Now this touches on the much-discussed question within the Platonic tradition – of which there is an extended account, for example, in Proclus' *Commentary on the Parmenides* (Book 3, cols. 815–33) – namely, of what things there are Forms, though Proclus does not there broach the question of Forms of opposites. The existence of Forms of Evils is dismissed, as are those of Forms of artificial objects and of individuals, but there is no discussion of such opposites as black and white, light and dark, or hot and cold. So Plutarch's postulation of a Form of Cold is not necessarily unorthodox.[26]

However, my concern is rather with the manner in which he advances his various solutions to the *problêma*, since they are couched in terms of increasing levels of *pithanotês*. First (946A), there is a brief listing of arguments in favour of cold being simply a *sterêsis*; but these are quickly countered (946B–948A) by a series of considerations in

---

[24] In this I am much indebted to the most useful discussion of George Boys-Stones (1997).

[25] Favorinus is an interesting figure in many ways, which need not be gone into here. Jan Opsomer devotes a good discussion to him in Chapter 5 of *In Search of the Truth*, being himself indebted to an essay by Anna Maria Ioppolo (1993), in which she shows that, contrary to the intemperate allegations of Galen in his treatise *De Optima Doctrina*, Favorinus was actually most probably a sceptic of the Carneadic persuasion. Cf. also Charles Brittain (2007), who provides a good discussion also of Plutarch, and of Numenius; and Mauro Bonazzi (2003), pp. 158–70.

[26] To be fair to Plutarch, he nowhere speaks of Cold as being a Form, but rather a *dynamis* and an *ousia*, which is compatible with its being merely an essential quality of one of the elemental Forms.

favour of its being a positive *dynamis* of some sort. I give, as a sample, the beginning of Plutarch's counter-attack (946B–C):[27]

> First of all, must we not be wary of one point in this argument (sc. that cold is simply the *sterêsis* of heat)? It eliminates many obvious forces (*dynameis*) by considering them not to be qualities or properties, but merely the negation of qualities or properties, weight being the negation of lightness and hardness that of softness, black that of white, and bitter that of sweet, and so in any other case where there is a natural opposition of forces rather than a relation of positive and negative.
>
> Another point is that all negation is inert and unproductive: blindness, for instance, and deafness, silence or death. Here you have defections of definite forms (*eidê*) and the annihilation of realities (*ousiai*), not things that are of themselves natures (*physeis*) or realities. It is the nature of coldness, however, to produce affects and alterations (*pathê kai metabolai*) in bodies that it enters no less than those caused by heat. Many objects can be frozen solid, or become condensed, or made viscous, by cold. Moreover, the property whereby coldness promotes rest and resists motion is not inert, but acts by pressure and resistance, being endowed with a constrictive and preservative tension (*tonos*).

We see here counter-arguments being brought to bear against an initial assertion, 'Cold is a mere absence of heat', very much in the manner of a Socratic *elenchus*. This position continues to be established, with further plausible arguments, over the next few chapters (3–7), until, in ch. 8 (948A–B), we are in a position to advance to the next stage: if cold is a positive *dynamis*, while being the opposite of heat, which is a *dynamis* of the element Fire, then to which of the other three elements might it best be related?

This initiates a three-part enquiry, which once again could be reconstructed as a Socratic dialogue – one thinks of something like the successive candidates for knowledge in the *Theaetetus*. Plutarch proposes to take in turn the three other elements, Air, Water and Earth, each of which might be opposed, with varying degrees of plausibility, to Fire, and examine their claims to be the principle of Cold. At the outset, in ch. 9, he identifies the proponents of the

---

[27] I borrow the Loeb translation of Cherniss & Helmbold, *Moralia* 12 (Cambridge, MA, 1927), slightly emended.

candidature of Air as the Stoics (thus putting them nicely in their place as the proponents of the least plausible alternative), those of Water as the rather motley combination of the Presocratic sage Empedocles and the Peripatetic Strato of Lampsacus, while he leaves Earth, as the third candidate, for the moment without a champion.

All three candidates, of course, have something to be said for them, but then again, the first two have much to be said against them. The case of air is proposed, with various persuasive arguments, in chs. 9–12, rounded off by this significant address to Favorinus (949F):

> So now, Favorinus, the argument that attributes the primal force of cold to the air depends on such plausibilities (*pithanotêtes*) as these.

We are then directed to Water, the case for which is set out in chs. 13–16, with many plausible arguments, at the end of which Favorinus is once again invited to weigh up the probabilities, while Plutarch moves him gently on to his final alternative (952C–D):

> Now you must pursue the subject by setting these arguments against their predecessors' (*skopei dê kai tauta paraballôn ekeinois*). For Chrysippus, thinking that the air is primordially cold because it is also dark, merely mentioned those who affirm that water is at a greater distance from the aether than is air; and wishing to make them some answer, he said, 'If so, we might as well declare that even earth is primordially cold because it is at the greatest distance from the aether' – tossing off this argument as if it were utterly inadmissible and absurd. But I have a mind to maintain that earth too is not destitute of probable and convincing arguments (*eikotes kai pithanoi [logoi]*).

– conjoining here, significantly, Plato's key term for the account of physical reality in the *Timaeus* (*eikôs logos*) with the favourite term of Carneades' epistemology. He then goes on to appropriate Chrysippus' identification of air as dark and cold with greater plausibility for earth (952D); and for the next five chapters (17–22) proceeds to develop a series of arguments in favour of the essential coldness of earth, ending with the following thoroughly Platonist flourish:

> We must, therefore, believe that the reason why the wise and learned men of old held that there is no mingling between earthly and celestial reality was not that they distinguished up and down by relative

position, as we do in the case of scales; but rather it was the difference in powers that led them to assign such things as are hot and bright, swift and buoyant, to the immortal and eternal nature, while darkness and cold and slowness they considered the unhappy heritage of perishable and submerged beings (*phthitoi kai eneroi*).[28] Then too, the body of a living creature, as long as it breathes and flourishes, does, as the poets say, enjoy both warmth and life; but when these forsake it and it is abandoned in the realm of earth alone, immediately frigidity and congelation seize upon it, since warmth naturally resides in anything else rather than the earthy.[29]

Having thus laid out in order the arguments in favour of air, water and earth, with a certain bias towards the claims of earth, Plutarch ends with what seems to me to be a teasing and light-hearted flourish directed at his former pupil, recognizing his championing of the sceptical tradition of the New Academy, and encouraging him to stick to it (955A):

> Compare these arguments, Favorinus, with the pronouncements of others; and if they neither fall short or much exceed them in plausibility, then say farewell to opinions (*doxai*), being convinced as you are that it is more philosophic to suspend judgement (*epekhein*) in face of things that are unclear (*adêla*) than to grant assent (*synkatatithesthai*) to them.

What we seem to have here, then, is a dialectical fugue played by Plutarch, for the delectation of Favorinus, and presumably any other sympathetic readers who might come upon it, on a theme concerning a representative problem related to the physical world, showing how a Platonist with loyalties both to the New Academy and to the Old might approach it. I choose it, not because it seems to me to embody Plutarch's most serious philosophizing,[30] but rather because it demonstrates rather well his dexterity in manipulating the full extent

---

[28] A suggestion here, perhaps, with this latter term, which denotes properly the ghosts of the dead or gods of the underworld, of the notion that the sublunary world is the Hades of the poets, as Plutarch was on occasion prepared to maintain (cf. *De gen. Socr.* 591A–B).

[29] I borrow the Loeb translation of Cherniss & Helmbold, *Moralia* 12 (Cambridge, MA, 1927), slightly emended.

[30] In fact, as is argued persuasively by George Boys-Stones ((1997a), p. 237), Plutarch probably feels that he has made a good case for earth, his arguments being based on Plato's theory of the basic triangles and elemental bodies as laid out in *Ti.* 55D–56B. I feel, therefore, that this is an aspect of the ironic and teasing quality of this treatise.

of the tradition which he saw himself as inheriting. He would be prepared to accept that *aporia* lies at the core of true philosophy, while not being incompatible with dogmatism as regards first principles, and the acceptance of a realm of true being superior, and largely antithetical, to the sublunary, material world; and this, I believe, he felt was also true of the chief figures within the New-Academic tradition, Arcesilaus and Carneades.

Conclusion

This little work, as specified at the outset, does not aspire to be a comprehensive account of the origins and development of the Platonist tradition, but rather has the more modest aim – befitting its origin as a set of lectures – of providing a series of studies of salient features of that tradition. If we recall once again the ingenious definition of 'Ur-Platonism' provided by Lloyd Gerson in his insightful study, *From Plato to Platonism,* mentioned in the Introduction, as a combination of negativities, specifically: anti-materialism, anti-mechanism, anti-nominalism, anti-relativism and anti-scepticism, I can formulate my purpose here as being to demonstrate how, without at all abandoning those principles, Platonists after Plato proceeded to construct a series of positive positions, in the areas of metaphysics, ethics and epistemology, on their basis.

To take metaphysical issues first, Platonism is obviously committed to metaphysical dualism, as postulating a 'real' world of immaterial Forms and immortal souls, presided over by the principles of the One and the Indefinite Dyad, while not in general succumbing, except in the later cases of Plutarch and Numenius, to the temptations of ethical dualism – despite apparent gestures in that direction by Plato in various passages.

Apart from the issue of the overall governance of the universe, the exact status and situation of the system of Forms would seem to be a key issue for the tradition, and, by reason of Plato's penchant for deviousness in exposition and tendency to resort to mythologizing when presenting doctrines of major importance, that question has remained a long-standing conundrum in Platonic scholarship, which I have long been concerned to unravel. I have made an attempt at it here, which may or may not prove persuasive.

In the sphere of ethics, less contentiously, we can see a broadly body- and world-negating system arising, which sets a premium on the withdrawal of the soul from dependence on, or contact with, the desires and concerns of the body, or 'goods' of the external world, while at the same time never assenting to the extreme position taken up later by the Stoics, of the complete rejection of bodily and external goods. These were always recognized as 'lower' or 'contingent' goods by Platonists, never just as 'indifferents'; nor was it judged necessary to strive to extirpate the passions (*apatheia*), but merely to moderate them (*metriopatheia*) – though quite a range of positions could be taken up within that broad spectrum! The dominant version of the *telos*, or 'purpose of life', came to be identified as 'assimilation to God' (*homoiôsis theôi*), as opposed to the Stoic ideal of 'conformity to Nature' – though, as we have seen, a figure such as Antiochus of Ascalon could be content with the latter, with modifications.

Lastly, despite the apparent adoption of scepticism by the 'New Academy', I have sought to explore how they could be – and were, by such a figure as Plutarch – embraced within the broader Platonist tradition, by according due weight to the Socratic strand within that tradition. Indeed, Arcesilaus and Carneades can be seen as really taking aim at the Stoic assertion that certainty (*katalêpsis*) can be attained in the material realm, through the senses, which is a claim that Plato himself would have taken issue with as well. Indeed, it is significant that Sextus Empiricus, the great champion of scepticism, does not regard the Academics as true sceptics at all, compared with his hero, Pyrrho. So the New Academy may be accepted, I think, though with some reservations, as constituting part of the Platonist tradition as a whole, as may the broader aporetic tradition, represented by Plutarch himself in many of his works.

Bibliography

Allen, J. 1994. 'Academic Probabilism and Stoic Epistemology', *Classical Quarterly* 44, pp. 85–113.

Alline, H. 1915. *Histoire du texte de Platon*, Paris.

Annas, J. 1988. 'The Heirs of Socrates', *Phronesis* 33, pp. 100–12.

　　1992. 'Plato the Sceptic' in *OSAP Supplementary Vol. 1992: Methods of Interpreting Plato and His Dialogues*, pp. 43–72.

　　1999. *Platonic Ethics, Old and New*, Ithaca.

Babut, D. 1994. 'Du scepticisme au dépassement de la raison. Philosophie et foi réligieuse chez Plutarque' in *Parerga: choix d'articles de Daniel Babut (1974–1994)*, Lyon, pp. 549–84.

　　2007. 'L'unité de l'Académie selon Plutarque. Notes en marge d'un débat ancien et toujours actuel', in Bonazzi, M., Lévy, C. & Steel, C. (eds.), *A Platonic Pythagoras: Platonism and Pythagoreanism in the Imperial Age*, Turnhout, pp. 63–98.

Baltzly, D. 2004. 'The Virtues and "Becoming like God": Alcinous to Proclus', *OSAP* 26, pp. 297–321.

Barnes, J. 1989. 'Antiochus of Ascalon' in Griffin & Barnes (eds.) (1989), pp. 51–96.

Bett, R. 1989. 'Carneades' *Pithanon*: A Reappraisal of its Role and Status', *OSAP* 7, pp. 59–94.

　　1990. 'Carneades' Distinction between Assent and Approval', *Monist* 73, pp. 3–20.

　　(ed.). 2010. *The Cambridge Companion to Ancient Scepticism*, Cambridge.

Bobonich, C. 2002. *Plato's Utopia Recast*, Oxford.

Bonazzi, M. 2003. *Academici e Platonici. Il dibattito antico sullo scetticismo di Platone*, Milan.

　　2006. 'Continuité et rupture dans l'Académie et le platonisme', *Etudes platoniciennes* III, pp. 231–44.

　　2014. 'Plutarch and the Sceptics' in Beck, M. (ed.), *A Companion to Plutarch*, Chichester, pp. 121–34.

Boys-Stones, G. 1997a. 'Plutarch on the Probable Principle of Cold: Epistemology and the *De Primo Frigido*', *Classical Quarterly* 47, pp. 227–38.

1997b. 'Thyrsus-Bearer of the Academy or Enthusiast for Plato? Plutarch's *De Stoicorum Repugnantiis*' in Mossman, J. (ed.), *Plutarch and His Intellectual World*, London, pp. 41–58.

Brittain, C. 2007. 'Middle Platonists on Academic Scepticism' in Sharples, R.W. & Sorabji, R. (eds.). *Greek and Roman Philosophy 100 B.C.–200 CE*, London, Vol. II, pp. 297–315.

Burnyeat, M. 1980. 'Can the Sceptic Live His Scepticism?' in Schofield, M., Burnyeat, M. & Barnes, J. (1980), pp. 117–48 (repr. in Burnyeat 2012).

(ed.). 1983. *The Sceptical Tradition*, Berkeley/Los Angeles.

Campbell, L. 1883. *The Theaetetus of Plato*, Oxford.

Cherniss, H. 1954. "The Sources of Evil According to Plato', *Proceedings of the American Philosophical Society* 98, pp. 23–30.

Cornford, F.M. 1935. *Plato's Theory of Knowledge*, London.

Couissin, P. 1929. 'Le stoicisme de la Nouvelle Académie', *Revue d'histoire de la philosophie* 3, pp. 241–76.

Dillon, J. 1977. *The Middle Platonists*, London/Ithaca (2nd ed. 1996).

1983. 'Plotinus, Philo and Origen on the Grades of Virtue', in Blume, H.-D. & Mann, F. (eds.), *Platonismus und Christentum*, Münster, pp. 92–105.

1984. 'Speusippus in Iamblichus', *Phronesis* 29, pp. 325–32.

1986. 'Xenocrates' Metaphysics: Fr. 15 (Heinze) Re-examined', *Ancient Philosophy* 5, pp. 47–52.

1990. *The Golden Chain; Studies in the Development of Platonism and Christianity*, Aldershot.

1993. *Alcinous, The Handbook of Platonism*, Oxford.

1996. 'An Ethic for the Late Antique Sage', in Gerson, L.P. (ed.), *The Cambridge Companion to Plotinus*, Cambridge, pp. 315–35.

1997a. *The Great Tradition: Further Studies in the Development of Platonism and Early Christianity*, Aldershot.

1997b. 'The Riddle of the *Timaeus:* Is Plato Sowing Clues?', in Joyal, M. (ed.), *Studies in Plato and the Platonic Tradition: Essays Presented to John Whittaker*, pp. 25–42 (repr. in Dillon 2012).

1999. 'Plutarch's Debt to Xenocrates' in Perez Jimenez, A. et al. (eds.), *Plutarco, Platon y Aristoteles: Actas del V Congreso internacional de la I.P. S.*, Madrid, pp. 305–11 (repr. in Dillon (2012)).

2002a. 'Plutarch on God; Theodicy and Cosmogony in the Thought of Plutarch' in Frede & Laks (eds.) (2002), pp. 223–38.

2002b. 'Theophrastus' Critique of the Old Academy in the *Metaphysics*' in Fortenbaugh, W.W. & Wöhrle, G. (eds.), *On the Opuscula of Theophrastus*, Stuttgart, pp. 175–87 (repr. in Dillon 2012).

2003. *The Heirs of Plato: A Study of the Old Academy (347–274 BCE)*, Oxford.

2012. *The Platonic Heritage: Further Studies in the History of Platonism and Early Christianity*, Farnham.

Donini, P.L. 2002. 'L'eredità academica e i fondamenti del platonismo in Plutarco' in Barbanti, M. & Romano, F. (eds.), *Henosis kai Philia: Unione e amicizia. Omaggio a Francesco Romano*, Catania, pp. 247–73 (repr. in Donini, P.L., *Commentary and Tradition: Aristotelianism, Platonism and Post-Hellenistic Philosophy*, Berlin, 2010).

Dorandi, T. 2007. *Nell' officina dei classici*, Rome.

Duerlinger J. 1985. 'Ethics and the Divine Life in Plato's Philosophy', *Journal of Religious Ethics*, 13, pp. 312–31.

Ferrari, F. 1995. *Dio, idée e materia: la struttura del cosmo in Plutarco di Cheronea*, Naples.

Forster, M. 2006. 'Socrates' Demand for Definitions', *OSAP* 31, pp. 1–47.

2007. 'Socrates' Profession of Ignorance', *OSAP* 32, pp. 1–35.

Frede, D. & Laks, A. (eds.) 2002. *Traditions of Theology: Studies in Hellenistic Theology, Its Background and Aftermath*, Leiden.

Frede, M. 1979. 'The Sceptic's Beliefs' (originally 'Des Skeptikers Meinungen', *Neue Hefte für Philosophie* 15–16, pp. 102–29, in Frede 1987).

1983/1987. 'Stoics and Sceptics on Clear and Distinct Impressions' in Burnyeat (1983), repr. in Frede (1987).

1987. *Essays in Ancient Philosophy*, Oxford.

Gerson, L. 2013. *From Plato to Platonism*, Ithaca.

Göransson, T. 1995. *Albinus, Alcinous, Arius Didymus*, Göteborg.

Görgemanns, H. 1960. *Beiträge zur Interpretation von Platons Nomoi*, München.

Griffin, M. & Barnes, J. (eds.) 1989. *Philosophia Togata: Essays on Philosophy and Roman Society I*, Oxford.

Griswold C. (ed.) 1988. *Platonic Writings, Platonic Readings*, London.

Halfwassen, J. 2012. 'Monism and Dualism in Plato's Doctrine of Principles' in Nikulin, D. (ed.), *The Other Plato: the Tübingen Interpretation of Plato's Inner-Academic Teachings*, Binghamton, pp. 143–59.

Hirzel, R. 1877–83. *Untersuchungen zu Cicero's philosophischen Schriften III*, Leipzig.

Inwood, B. 2014. 'Ancient Goods: the *tria genera bonorum* in Ethical Theory', in Lee, M.K. (ed.), *Strategies of Argument. Essays in Ancient Ethics, Epistemology and Logic*, New York & Oxford, pp. 255–80.

Ioppolo, A.M. 1986. *Opinione e scienza: Il dibattito tra Stoici e Accademici nel III e nel II secolo a.C.*, Naples.

1993. 'The Academic Position of Favorinus of Arelate', *Phronesis* 38, pp. 183–213.

Krämer, H.-J. 1964. *Der Ursprung der Geistmetaphysik: Untersuchungen zur Geschichte der platonischen Ontologie zwischen Platon und Plotin*, Amsterdam.

Levett, M.J. 1990. *The Theaetetus of Plato*, Indianapolis.

Lévy, C. 2010. 'The Sceptical Academy: Decline and Afterlife' in Bett (ed.) (2010), pp. 81–104.

Long, A.A. 1967. 'Carneades and the Stoic Telos', *Phronesis* 12, pp. 59–90.

1974. *Hellenistic Philosophy*, London/New York.

1988. 'Socrates in Hellenistic Philosophy', *Classical Quarterly* 38, pp. 150–71.

Long, A.A. & Dillon, J.M. (eds) 1988. *The Question of 'Eclecticism': Studies in Later Greek Philosophy*, Berkeley/Los Angeles.

McDowell, J. 1973. *Plato. Theaetetus*, Oxford.

Mann, W. 2006. 'Plato in Tübingen: A Discussion of Konrad Gaiser, *Gesammelte Schriften*', *OSAP* 31, pp. 349–400.

Matthews. G.B. 1999. *Socratic Perplexity and the Nature of Philosophy*, Oxford.

Merki, H. 1952. *Homoiosis theôi: Von der platonischen Angleichung an Gott zur Gottänlichkeit bei Gregor von Nyssa*, Freiburg.

Merlan, P. 1960. *From Platonism to Neoplatonism*, The Hague.

Meyers, B.E. & E.P. Sanders (eds.) 1982. *Self-Definition in the Greco-Roman World*, London/Philadelphia.

Michalewski, A. 2014. *La puissance de l'intelligible: la théorie plotinienne des Formes au miroir de l'héritage medioplatonicienne*, Leuven.

Nehamas, A. 1998. *The Art of Living: Socratic Reflections from Plato to Foucault*. Berkeley/Los Angeles.

Opsomer, J. 1998. *In Search of the Truth: Academic Tendencies in Middle Platonism*, Brussels.

Politis, V. 2015. *The Structure of Enquiry in Plato's Early Dialogues*. Cambridge.

Press, G. 2000. *Who Speaks for Plato? Studies in Platonic Anonymity*, Lanham, MD.

Radice, R. 1989. *Platonismo e creazionismo in Filone di Alessandria*, Milan.

Rich, A., 1954. 'The Platonic Ideas as the Thoughts of God', *Mnemosyne* ser. 4, 7, pp. 123–33.

Roloff, D. 1970. *Gottänlichkeit, Vergöttlichung und Erhöhung zu seligem Leben: Untersuchungen zur Herkunft der platonischen Angleichung an Gott*, Berlin.

Rowett, C. 2014. *Knowledge and Truth in Plato*, Oxford.

Schibli, H. 'Xenocrates' Daemons and the Irrational Soul', *Classical Quarterly* 43, pp. 143–67.

Schofield, M., Burnyeat, M. & Barnes, J. (eds.) 1980. *Doubt and Dogmatism*, Oxford.

Sedley, D. 1996. 'Three Platonist Interpretations of the *Theaetetus*' in
    Gill, C. & McCabe, M.M. (eds.), *Form and Argument in Late Plato*,
    Oxford, pp. 79–103.
  1999. 'The Ideal of Godlikeness' in Fine, G. (ed.), *Oxford Readings in
    Plato: Ethics, Politics, Religion and the Soul*, Oxford, pp. 309–28.
  2002. 'The Origins of Stoic God', in Frede & Laks (eds.) (2002), pp.
    41–83.
  (ed.) 2012. *The Philosophy of Antiochus*, Cambridge.
Stough, C. 1969. *Greek Scepticism*, Berkeley/Los Angeles.
Striker, G. 1980. 'Sceptical Strategies' in Schofield et al. (eds.) (1980), pp.
    54–83 (repr. in Striker 1996).
  1996. *Essays on Hellenistic Epistemology and Ethics*, Cambridge.
Swanton, C. 2003. *Virtue Ethics, a Pluralistic View*, Oxford.
Tarán, L. 1975. Academica: *Plato, Philip of Opus and the Pseudo-Platonic
    Epinomis*, Philadelphia.
Tarrant, H. 1985. *Scepticism or Platonism?* Cambridge.
  1995. 'Counting Plato's Principles' in Ayres, L. (ed.), *The Passionate
    Intellect: Essays on the Transformation of Classical Traditions*, New
    Brunswick/ London, pp. 67–82.
  2007. 'Moral Goal and Moral Virtues in Middle Platonism' in
    Sharples, R.W. & Sorabji, R. (eds.), *Greek Philosophy 100 BCE–200
    CE*, London, Vol. II, pp. 419–29.
Theiler, W. 1930. *Die Vorbereitung des Neuplatonismus*, Berlin.
Thorsrud, H. 2010. 'Arcesilaus and Carneades', in Bett (ed.) (2010), pp.
    58–80.
Vlastos, G. 1991. *Socrates, Ironist and Moral Philosopher*, Cambridge.
  1994. *Socratic Studies*, ed. M. Burnyeat, Cambridge.
Warren, J. 2002. 'Socratic Scepticism in Plutarch's *Adversus Colotem*',
    Elenchos 23, pp. 333–56.

Index Locorum

General Index

Printed in the United States
by Baker & Taylor Publisher Services